NEW ENGLAND REMEMBERS

Sacco & Vanzetti

Eli C. Bortman

Robert J. Allison, Series Editor

Commonwealth Editions
Beverly, Massachusetts

ISBN-13: 978-1-889833-76-7
ISBN-10: 1-889833-76-2

Library of Congress Cataloging-in-Publication Data
Bortman, Eli C.
  Sacco and Vanzetti / Eli Bortman.
    p. cm. — (New England remembers)
  Includes index.
  ISBN 1-889833-76-2
  1. Sacco, Nicola, 1891–1927—Trials, litigation, etc. 2. Vanzetti, Bartolomeo, 1888–1927—Trials, litigation, etc. 3. Trials (Murder)—Massachusetts. I. Title. II. Series.
  KF224.S2B665 2005
  345.73'02523'09744—dc22   2004026443

Cover and interior design by Laura McFadden, laura.mcfadden@rcn.com.

Printed in the United States.

Commonwealth Editions
266 Cabot Street, Beverly, Massachusetts 01915
www.commonwealtheditions.com

Front cover photo: Sacco and Vanzeetti in handcuffs, courtesy of Bettmann/Corbis
Back cover photo: Funeral procession, courtesy of the Massachusetts Archives

New England Remembers series
Robert J. Allison, Series Editor
The Hurricane of 1938
The Big Dig
The Cocoanut Grove Fire
Lizzie Borden

The "New England Remembers" logo features a photo of the Thomas Pickton House, Beverly, Massachusetts, used courtesy of the Beverly Historical Society.

CONTENTS

FOREWORD

THEY WERE TWO ITALIAN IMMIGRANTS, arrested, convicted, and executed for a crime they most likely did not commit. Nicola Sacco and Bartolomeo Vanzetti, a factory worker and a fish-peddler, anonymous beyond a small circle of friends, family, and anarchist allies, by 1927 were the center of an international movement to spare their lives and indict the system that sent them to their deaths.

Who were Sacco and Vanzetti? Why did so many prominent Americans—including poet Edna St. Vincent Millay, novelists Upton Sinclair and John Dos Passos, lawyer Felix Frankfurter—champion their cause? Why was it so important to Massachusetts that Sacco and Vanzetti be executed?

After being sentenced to die, Vanzetti said that had he not been falsely charged in a Christmas Eve robbery in Bridgewater, "I might have lived out my life, talking at street corners to scorning men." He would have lived and died, "unmarked, unknown, a failure. Now we are not a failure." They had succeeded in their work "for tolerance, for justice, for man's understanding of man. . . . Our words—our lives—our pains—nothing! The taking of our lives—lives of a good shoemaker and a poor fish-peddler—all! The last moment belongs to us—the agony is our triumph!"

The deaths of Sacco and Vanzetti did not lead to an anarchist revolution, but their struggle against the Massachusetts judicial system sparked a movement to restrain the arbitrary power of biased judges. Lawyer Eli Bortman in this book examines the lives, the deaths, and the legacies of these two men, and shows why New England remembers Nicola Sacco and Bartolomeo Vanzetti.

Robert J. Allison, Series Editor
Boston, Massachusetts

The Arrest,
and Its Context

Shortly after ten on the night of May 5, 1920, two police officers boarded a trolley in Brockton, Massachusetts. The chief of police in neighboring Bridgewater had asked them to look for two suspicious-looking foreigners, who were coming on a trolley from Bridgewater. He said the men were wanted in connection with a stolen car investigation.

The policemen did find two foreign men—Nicola Sacco and Bartolomeo Vanzetti on the trolley, and brought them to the Brockton Police Headquarters. When the police searched them, they found that each man was carrying a loaded handgun. In addition, Sacco was carrying a handwritten notice of an upcoming anarchist rally:

Proletarians, you have fought all the wars. You have worked for all the owners. . . . Have you harvested the fruits of your labors, the price of your victories? Does the present smile on you? Does the future promise you anything? Have you found a piece of land on which you can live like a human being and die like a human being? On these questions . . . the struggle for existence, Bartolomeo Vanzetti will speak. . . .

Bridgewater's police chief, Michael Stewart, who had asked the Brockton police to look for the two men, was actually investigating a different crime. Three weeks earlier, in Braintree, Massachusetts, several armed gunmen had robbed and murdered a payroll clerk and his guard, getting away with $15,776. Chief Stewart arrived at the Brockton police station shortly before midnight on May 5, and he questioned first Vanzetti and then Sacco separately. He did not tell them why they had been picked up, but he did ask them where they had been, why they had gone there, whether they had seen two men on a motorcycle, and why they were carrying guns. Then Stewart abruptly changed the focus of his questions, and began asking them about their political beliefs.

Were they Socialists? Anarchists? Communists? Members of the Industrial Workers of the World (IWW)? Did they subscribe to anarchist literature? Did they belong to any anarchist clubs? Were they American citizens? Did they support the government here? Did they advocate the overthrow of the government?

When Stewart asked the quiet, intense Vanzetti where he and Sacco had been going, Vanzetti said they were going to visit a friend of his, a man he knew only as "Poppy." He did not know the man's real name or where he lived. They could not find him, realized it was too late to visit once they had reached Bridgewater, and so were heading home. Why was he carrying a gun? Vanzetti said he needed it as protection in his business, which was peddling fish in Plymouth.

Pursuing a new lead on the Braintree murders, Stewart was looking for Mike Boda, the owner of a Buick being repaired at Simon Johnson's garage, and had alerted Johnson to call him when anyone came to claim it. When four men came to Johnson's house on the evening of May 5 (his garage, next door to his house, was closed), Johnson's wife, Ruth, went next door to the neighbors to call the police. Two of the men, Mike Boda and Ricardo Orciani, had come on Orciani's motorcycle; two of the others had arrived on foot. Johnson told them the car did not have a current license plate, and that they really should come back with a plate before they took the car. The men seemed to agree, and they left without the car. By the time the police arrived, all four were gone. Boda had left on the motorcycle; the police guessed that the two on foot had boarded the Brockton-bound street-car that passed in front of the Johnson house at 9:40.

Now the Brockton police had two men in custody. Chief Stewart brought Johnson, the garage owner, with him when he went to the

Brockton police station, and Johnson told Stewart that Sacco and Vanzetti were two of the men who had been at his house earlier that evening. So when Sacco and Vanzetti each told Stewart that they had not been at Johnson's house, and that they had not seen a motorcycle, Stewart thought he needed to see where his questions might lead. When they couldn't tell Stewart any more about the mysterious Poppy—where he lived or what his full name was—and why they were visiting him, he grew more suspicious.

The Brockton police charged both men with carrying weapons illegally—Sacco was carrying a Colt pistol and thirty-two cartridges, and Vanzetti a Harrington & Richardson revolver and some shotgun shells. They were held in the police station overnight. The next day, Norfolk County's district attorney, Frederick G. Katzmann, arrived to question them.

Katzmann's questions, however, focused not so much on the guns the two men had been carrying, as on the political notice Sacco had had. In fact, the two men were supporters of the growing anarchist movement, and were planning a rally in Brockton to raise money for the defense of other anarchists. Based on the line of police questioning—and now the D.A.'s questions—Sacco and Vanzetti now believed they had been apprehended not only because they were foreigners but because they were anarchists.

SACCO AND VANZETTI HAD BOTH left peasant families in Italy to look for better opportunities in the United States, and both arrived in 1908, though they would not meet until 1917. Bartolomeo Vanzetti, born in 1888 and the oldest of four children, came from the northern Piedmont region of Italy. Although his family owned a farm, he was apprenticed at age thirteen to work in a bakery. Several years as a baker or candy maker led to stretches of serious respiratory illnesses, and during periods of recuperation he read anticlerical and radical pamphlets and began thinking about the exploitation of the working class. Realizing that the hard life in Italian bakeries and kitchens would kill him, he decided to seek a new life in America.

From New York, Vanzetti set out on a string of menial jobs, from washing dishes to working in a brickyard, a stone quarry, an iron foundry, on railroad tracks, and on various construction projects between New York and New England. In 1913 he was renting a room in Plymouth, Massachusetts, where he worked for a while at the Plymouth Cordage Works, loading coils of rope onto railroad cars. His landlord, Vincenzo Brini, was not only an immigrant and an anarchist, but, like Vanzetti, was a supporter of the *Cronaca Sovversiva* (Subversive Chronicle), an anarchist paper published by Luigi Galleani.

Vanzetti's itinerant employment supported his reading and his developing ideas. He read a wide variety of history, philosophy, and literature, and thought deeply about both what he read and what he experi-

Bartolomeo Vanzetti (courtesy of the Massachusetts Archives)

enced in his working life. Vanzetti's views on anarchism had begun to gel in 1912, when he first read a copy of Galleani's *Cronaca Sovversiva*. Galleani, who had come to America in 1901, had moved his paper in 1912 from Barre, Vermont, to Lynn, Massachusetts. Galleani used *Cronaca Sovversiva*, as well as his fiery speeches, to spell out his basic anarchist philosophy: eliminating all economic, political, and religious institutions, establishing instead a society based on mutual aid. Because the state and the capitalists did not hesitate to use violence against workers, Galleani saw violence—including bombs and assassinations—as "propaganda by the deed," and a legitimate means to achieve the desired end. *La Salute e in voi!* ("Health is in you!"), Galleani's 1905 bomb-making manual, was advertised in the *Cronaca Sovversiva* as "an indispensable pamphlet for all comrades who love self-instruction" (though the *Cronaca* later had to warn users about an error in the recipe for nitroglycerine). The years from the beginning of World War I to the time of Sacco and Vanzetti's arrest were marked with unrest and hostility. Various anarchist groups became active, and engaged in seemingly senseless acts of violence. For example, in 1914, anarchists in New York tried to blow up John D. Rockefeller's home in Tarrytown (three anarchists blew themselves up instead), and others planted bombs that exploded in St. Patrick's Cathedral, the Church of St. Alphonsus, the Bronx Courthouse, and beneath the police court in the Tombs. On December 17, 1916, an anarchist bomb damaged a police station in Boston's North End.

Vanzetti saw a difference between socialism and anarchism. Socialists simply wanted a different form of government, while anarchists wanted neither a state nor a government. He thought that the working class should "smash all the powers against it, not create a power for itself." He visualized a world of "free towns administered by their citizens" in which "mutual aid and co operation shall be the very base of a completely new social system."

In 1916 the workers in the cordage plant abruptly went on strike. The war in Europe had increased the demand for the cordage company's rope, and the workers—who were not unionized—wanted more than their $9 per week for a fifty-hour work week. (Women were paid $6 per week.) Although Vanzetti had already quit his job there, he walked the picket line, raised money for the strikers, made speeches, and even organized a parade in support of the strike. He reported on the strike's progress for the *Cronaca Sovversiva*, and when the American Federation of Labor and the IWW tried to organize the workers, Vanzetti argued against unionization in the paper—he saw union officials equally as authoritarian as management. Only the workers themselves could bring about real change.

NICOLA SACCO, BORN IN 1891 to a relatively prosperous farming family in the south of Italy, was the third son among seventeen children. Young Fernando, as he was then called (he adopted the name Nicola, after a cousin, when he fled to Mexico in 1917), preferred working with the farm machinery to toiling in the fields, and saw America as a place to pursue his mechanical interests. With his older brother Sabino, he set sail for the United States in 1908.

The Sacco brothers landed in Boston and settled in the Italian immigrant community in Milford, a small town twenty-five miles to the southwest. Sabino returned to Italy after a year, but Nicola got a job in a shoe factory and became a skilled craftsman, operating most of the shoemaking machinery. He soon earned forty to fifty dollars per week, and in 1912 married Rosina Zambelli, then seventeen. The next year Rosina gave birth to a son, Dante.

Although Sacco had a relatively good job and a comfortable family life, he was sensitive to the suffering of the working poor. He saw the contrast between their poverty and squalor and the wealth and comfort of the upper classes. The "injustice and cruel persecution in this free society of today, and specially for the poor people" troubled him, as he later wrote. He began to read socialist pamphlets and *Il Proletario*, an anarchist weekly newspaper. The passions of the 1912 textile strike in Lawrence, Massachusetts—which had erupted when factory owners there cut wages after the state forbid them from making their workers put in more than fifty-four hours a week—turned Sacco toward the anarchist movement. He began to attend meetings of a Milford anarchist group called Circolo di Studi Sociali. In this close-knit group Sacco met other anarchists, including Ricardo Orciani, with whom Mike Boda later drove to Johnson's garage. Sacco said that the Circolo di Studi Sociali members had "reciprocal love and sublime affection" for each other.

Like Vanzetti, Sacco subscribed to the *Cronaca Sovversiva* and contributed articles to it (he appealed for funds to aid strikers). He saw anarchism as a noble concept. One author has described him as "a man of few and relatively simple beliefs—capitalism is evil, government is slavery, war is a crime against humanity, freedom is essential for human development. . . . Anarchism . . . meant [a world with] no government, no police, no judges, no bosses, no authority; autonomous groups of people—the people own everything—work in cooperation—distribute by needs—equality, justice, comradeship—love each other." Sacco distributed anarchist literature and walked picket lines when other workers were on strike.

In 1916 iron miners in Minnesota's Mesabi Range went on strike. The IWW saw this as an opportunity to show its strength in the struggle between labor and management, and sent organizers to support the strikers. The mine owners hired a thousand armed guards to try to keep the mines working. Violent confrontations between picketers and these guards resulted in some deaths. Several IWW officials were charged with these homicides, even though they were not directly involved. Sacco raised money for the strikers and was arrested in a Milford demonstration in their support. Though Sacco was convicted and sentenced to three months in prison, the charges were dismissed on appeal. Shortly after his reprieve, personal tragedy struck as his second child, newborn daughter Alba, died. The *Cronaca Sovversiva* wrote in condolence that the baby girl had been spared "this wretched world, dripping in blood and degradation."

NICOLA SACCO AND BARTOLOMEO VANZETTI first met in Boston in the spring of 1917. The United States was about to enter the First World War, and Congress passed a conscription act in May 1917 requiring all men, citizens or not, to register for the draft by June 5. Galleani, in his *Cronaca Sovversiva*, urged his followers not to register, and if necessary to leave the country to avoid arrest for failure to register. Under the law, aliens were not subject to compulsory service, but could be arrested for failure to register. Ironically, Vanzetti was in the process of becoming an American citizen—he had applied on May 5, 1917.

Anarchists of the time, like other radicals, believed that the war would bring about the collapse of empires and capitalism; some, including Sacco and Vanzetti, hoped to return to Italy to advance the coming revolution. Galleanists gathered in Boston to plan a flight into Mexico, and Sacco and Vanzetti, as well as Mario Buda, or Mike Boda, were among thirty or so anarchists who formed a communal society in Monterrey, a town in northeastern Mexico. These men found life in Monterrey harder than they had expected, even harder than the peasant lives they had left in Italy. Most could not find work; those who could did odd jobs to support the others. Hungry and restless, within a few months they began to drift home.

Vanzetti and Sacco both returned to New England in September 1917. Vanzetti returned to Plymouth, working as a day laborer before buying a pushcart in January 1919 to peddle fish through the streets of

Niccola Sacco with his wife, Rosina, and son, Dante (courtesy of the Massachusetts Archives)

the town's Italian neighborhood. He sold fish by day and lectured on anarchism at night. Sacco reunited with Rosina and Dante, who had moved to Cambridge, and worked at a series of factory jobs over the next year. He quit one job when his employer urged him to buy a Liberty Bond to support the war. He refused: "I don't believe in war, and don't allow anyone to tell me how I spend my wages."

Jobs were difficult to come by, and at one point Rosina had to find work. But finally Sacco learned about the Three-K shoe factory in Stoughton, Massachusetts. One of the "Three K's" was Michael Kelley, who had taught Sacco edge-trimming nine years earlier at the Milford Shoe Company. Kelley, with his sons George and Leon (pictures of the "Three K's" were on the shoe boxes), had since started his own shoe factory. Sacco hired on with the Kelleys and even rented a house directly behind Michael Kelley's. At work and at home, he impressed his boss: "A good worker," Michael Kelley remembered. "Very steady. He never lost a day. . . . He was in early and stayed late. He was a great fellow to clean up everything." Kelley noted how carefully Sacco tended his garden—rising at four in the morning to work on his tomatoes, carrying buckets of water from the house during the dry season—before reporting to work at seven. It seemed an idyllic existence—Sacco and Rosina taking walks on Sundays with young Dante. Kelley entrusted Sacco with the keys to the factory, and his only concern was that Sacco was devoting a great deal of attention to the anarchist movement. A grandson of the Kelleys recalled a time Sacco distributed leaflets in the factory, and Michael and George reprimanded him—anxious both to keep order in their factory and to prevent their model employee's arrest. "Stop talking, Nick," George Kelley warned him, "till this time of antiradical excitement is past. You can't reform the world in a day." The Kelleys could not understand why Sacco, an ambitious, hard-working, and family centered man, would nor embrace the chance to do what they had as immigrants and secure a place in American society. "Give up the radical stuff! Be an American!" Michael Kelley would tell him.

Kelley was sensitive to the danger Sacco's beliefs posed to his future in the country. The Espionage Act of June 1917 allowed the post office to exclude from the mail any printed material encouraging resistance to federal laws, and its revision in the Sedition Act of May 1918 made it illegal to publish any "disloyal, profane, or scurrilous language" against the United States or its government. In October 1918 Congress passed the Immigration Act, allowing the deportation of alien anarchists.

Galleani had been arrested in June 1917 and interrogated about his anarchist views, but the government did not have enough evidence to deport him under the laws at that time. It did ban *Cronaca* from the mails, though, and in February and May of 1918 government officers raided the *Cronaca* offices. The May raid—conducted under the new Sedition Act—led to a roundup of eighty Galleanists.

The Immigration Act gave the government additional deportation powers. The prosecution no longer needed to prove that a defendant advocated violent overthrow of the government—an alien could be deported simply for belonging to an organization that advocated "opposition to all organized government." On the strength of this new law, in January 1919 the government ordered Galleani deported, although he wouldn't actually leave the country until May of that year.

The anarchist community reacted quickly to Galleani's deportation order. "GO AHEAD!" said a leaflet that appeared in New England in February 1919. "The senile fossils ruling the United States see red! Smelling their destruction, they have decided to check the storm by passing the Deportation law. . . . We, the American Anarchists, do not protest, for it is futile to waste any energy on feeble minded creatures led by His Majesty Phonograph Wilson." The leaflet warned: "You have shown no pity to us! We will do likewise." The page concluded, "And deport us! *We will dynamite you!*"

In February, Galleani spoke to an anarchist gathering in Taunton, Massachusetts, and the next night four anarchists who had attended the rally died while planting a bomb at the American Woolen Company (its workers were on strike) in Franklin. Late in April thirty package bombs were mailed to prominent citizens—including John D. Rockefeller, J. P. Morgan, Attorney General A. Mitchell Palmer, Secretary of Labor William B. Wilson (whose department oversaw deportation proceedings), Postmaster General Albert Burleson, the governors of Pennsylvania and Mississippi, the mayors of New York and Seattle, Supreme Court Justice Oliver Wendell Holmes, Jr. (who had ruled in favor of the 1918 Sedition Act, and upheld socialist leader Eugene Debs's conviction under the Espionage Act), Judge Kenesaw Mountain Landis, four senators, two congressmen, New York's police commissioner, several immigration officials, and the president of the American Woolen Company. Though the packages killed only one person—a maid who had opened it for her employer, former Georgia senator Thomas Hardwick, sponsor of a bill prohibiting foreign immigration—the authorities launched an immediate and thorough investigation into the package bombs. All the bombs were intended to arrive on May 1, and the list of victims was an anarchist's "who's who among exploiters."

Authorities feared that May 1—the Socialist holiday May Day—would be a day of general unrest. On that date there were riots at May Day parades—fights between radicals and patriotic citizens—leading to arrests of the radicals. But it was not until June 2, 1919, that more bombings hit New York, Boston, Paterson, New Jersey, Cleveland, Philadelphia, Pittsburgh, and Washington, D.C. Most sensationally, the home of Attorney General A. Mitchell Palmer was rocked by a blast at 11:15 P.M. Palmer was showered with broken glass, and though not injured, was badly shaken. His neighbor, Assistant Secretary of the Navy Franklin D. Roosevelt, recalled how the Quaker attorney general was "'theeing' and 'thouing' me all over the place—'thank thee, Franklin!' and all that." More shocking was the discovery that bits of the bomber were now scattered across the neighborhood—a piece of the left leg on the porch across the street, the spine smashing through a bedroom window, the scorched torso hanging on a house a block away, and a bit of scalp on a roof on S Street. At the time, authorities thought there were two bombers because so many fragments (and two hats) had been found at the scene. But subsequent investigation showed there was one bomber: Carlo Valdinoci, a publisher of Galleani's newspaper, the *Cronaca Sovversiva*. Valdinoci had been part of the Gruppo Autonomo, an Italian anarchist group in East Boston.

Bombs also damaged the Roxbury home of Judge Albert Hayden, who had handed down tough sentences for the May Day demonstrators, and the Newtonville home of state representative Leland Powers, sponsor of the state's antisedition act (which had become law on May 28) and son of the American Woolen Company's lawyer.

At each site, investigators found more anarchist leaflets. These were titled "Plain Words" and warned, "There will be bloodshed; we will not dodge; there will have to be murder; we will kill, because it is necessary; there will have to be destruction; we will destroy to rid the world of your tyrannical institutions." The document was signed, "THE ANARCHIST FIGHTERS."

The government responded quickly to this challenge. Attorney General Palmer needed little persuading that the anarchists posed a serious threat—he warned that revolution was "licking at the altars of the churches, leaping into the belfry of the school bell, crawling into the sacred corners of American homes, seeking to replace marriage vows with libertine laws, burning up the foundations of society." The morning after his house was blasted, he reorganized his department's antiradical squad, and within a few days he had increased the resources of the department's investigative bureau and put young investigator J. Edgar Hoover in charge of the General Intelligence Division (or Radical Division) of the Federal Bureau of Investigation.

In November, Palmer's Justice Department launched a series of raids on radicals—arresting more than three thousand foreigners and beginning deportation proceedings (ultimately some eight hundred would be expelled). Five hundred radicals were seized in Boston and held for deportation. While the "Palmer Raids" reassured some that the government would not tolerate its own destruction, others saw the raids as evidence that the government was becoming the oppressive monster the anarchists were warning about. Journalist H. L. Mencken, though not sympathetic to anarchists, called Palmer "the most eminent living exponent of cruelty, dishonesty, and injustice," and warned that the "system of espionage" he and his agents created was not matched "in the history of Russia, Austria, and Italy." Immigration commissioner Frederic Howe, who had received one of the mail bombs in April 1919, wrote that "the state not only abandoned the liberty which it should have protected, it lent itself to the stamping out of individualism and freedom." Proponents of due process of law formed the American Civil Liberties Union in response to the government's attack on constitutional guarantees.

Late in February 1920, agents in Brooklyn arrested two typesetters, Roberto Elia and Andrea Salsedo. Both were loyal Galleanists and had worked for the *Cronaca Sovversiva*, and in their printing shop police found paper and type that matched the "Plain Words" leaflets found at nearly every site in the June 1919 bombings. After several days of intensive interrogation, apparently including a severe beating, Salsedo confessed to printing the "Plain Words" flyer, and—in exchange for a promise of protection—identified other Galleanists.

In East Boston, members of the Gruppo Autonomo feared that the evidence Salsedo had revealed would implicate them in the 1919 bombings. Sacco, having learned at the same time that his mother had died in Italy, prepared for his own return home. On April 15 he traveled to the Italian consulate in Boston to secure passports for himself, the pregnant Rosina, and Dante. Vanzetti traveled to New York, where the Galleanists' new leader, Carlo Tresca (who had succeeded Galleani after his deportation), warned him that the Gruppo members should hide whatever anarchist literature they had. He reminded Vanzetti that under the 1918 Immigration Act mere possession of such materials was grounds for deportation. At their regular weekly meeting on May 2, 1920, Sacco, Vanzetti, and Orciani (now a Gruppo member) decided to contact Mike Boda, who owned a car, which they could borrow to collect the materials for safekeeping.

The members of the Gruppo also decided to hold a public meeting the following week, with Vanzetti as the speaker, to raise money to help with the legal bills of Elia and Salsedo. So it was that on the evening of May 5, 1920, Sacco, Vanzetti, Boda, and Orciani made their way to Bridgewater to pick up Mike Boda's car at Johnson's garage.

CHAPTER TWO

The Crime

Sacco and Vanzetti believed they had been arrested because they were anarchists. They knew the government was rounding up suspects in the wave of recent bombings, and they feared that Andrea Salsedo had given information on the Gruppo Autonomo's role. Sacco was already planning to leave the country—he had collected his tools from the Three-K factory, and he and Rosina and Dante would leave for New York on May 8. Vanzetti had told his father he had "saved up enough to be able to return to Italy in case the necessity to do so should arise." Others in their group had already been deported.

But their arrest on May 5 had nothing to do with the anarchist bombings. Instead, Chief Stewart had stumbled upon Sacco and Vanzetti while investigating the murder of a payroll clerk and security guard three weeks earlier in Braintree, Massachusetts.

AT ABOUT THREE IN THE AFTERNOON on Thursday, April 15, payroll clerk Frederick Parmenter of the Slater & Morrill shoe company in South Braintree, along with security guard Alessandro Berardelli, walked down Pearl Street from the company's office to its factory. Each carried a metal box—two feet long, one foot high, eight inches wide—filled with pay envelopes for the company's employees. Altogether, Parmenter and Berardelli had $15,776 in their boxes. Two men who had been leaning against a fence at the side of the street approached Parmenter and Berardelli as they passed the Rice & Hutchins shoe factory. One man grappled briefly with Berardelli and then shot him. Berardelli dropped his box and fell to the ground, and the gunman stood over him, shooting him several more times. As Parmenter turned to see what had happened, the other gunman shot him in the chest. Berardelli died immediately, and Parmenter died the next morning.

At the sound of gunshots a large touring car appeared, driving up Pearl Street slowly enough for a third man to jump out and help the other two robbers load the metal boxes into the car. The car drove off, a rifle pointed from the removed back window to ward off pursuers, as the robbers also threw bits of rubber hose studded with tacks onto the road to prevent a car chase.

It all had happened very quickly, but there were many eyewitnesses. One was on the street and had spoken to Parmenter just a minute before the shooting started. Several witnesses were working in the Slater & Morrill factory, at a workbench in front of an open window. A number of laborers were digging a foundation hole directly across the street from the factory, and saw the shooting. One witness came out of a poolroom on the next block when he heard the gunshots, and was in the street as the getaway car drove by. Several witnesses described the gunmen as "perhaps five feet six or seven, rather stocky." Estimates of their weights varied, but ranged from 140 to 160 pounds. Several said the gunmen were "of apparent Italian lineage." One man was said to be clean-shaven and wearing a cap. The other man had a mustache—closely cropped, said one witness—and wore a felt hat. The descriptions of the car also varied—some said it was black, others said that it was dark green, but everyone agreed it was a large touring car with curtains over the windows. One eyewitness who had been at his workbench in the factory recorded the license plate number. The police learned later that the plates had been stolen from a car parked in Needham. On the street the police were able to recover only some spent shells and a cloth cap.

Several witnesses told police they had noticed the black touring car going up and down Pearl Street earlier in the day, and gave various accounts of the appearance of the driver and passengers. One witness recalled having seen the car parked on Pearl Street before noon, with one man standing next to it and another underneath it, as if he was trying to repair it. Several witnesses had noticed two men leaning against the fence before the shooting started.

THE ROBBERY AND MURDERS of April 15, 1920, seemed related to a failed payroll robbery attempt the previous December. The day before Christmas in 1919, as a payroll truck approached the L. Q. White Company, a shoe factory in Bridgewater, Massachusetts, a car drove toward the truck on the wrong side of the street. Two armed men got out of the car and shouted to the truck's driver to stop. One of the gunmen fired several rounds from a shotgun. When the guard on the truck fired back the robbers apparently lost their nerve and fled on foot to the waiting getaway car. Several eyewitnesses described the three gunmen as "foreigners" and said the man with the shotgun had a dark complexion and a black mustache. Various eyewitnesses suggested that the robbers were Greek, Russian, Polish, Austrian, Italian, or Portuguese. One informant told police that the crime was the work of Italian anarchists who lived in a shack in the Bridgewater area; another believed the men were Russians from out of town.

While the witnesses could not narrow down the robbers' nationality, they did identify the getaway vehicle as a black touring car, either a Hudson or a Buick. One witness had recorded the car's license plate number. Police determined that these were dealer's plates issued to Hassam's Garage in nearby Needham. Two days after the robbery attempt—the day after Christmas—the police telephoned Hassam, who remembered that a few days earlier an Italian (with a dark complexion and a mustache) had visited his garage. The man said he had just bought a car and asked Hassam to lend him a set of plates. Hassam had refused. Now, after he hung up the phone, he looked in his garage and found that a set of his dealer's plates was missing. With this little bit of information to go on, the police did not launch a vigorous investigation.

Two days after the Braintree robbery and murders, on Saturday afternoon, April 17, two men riding horses in the woods of West

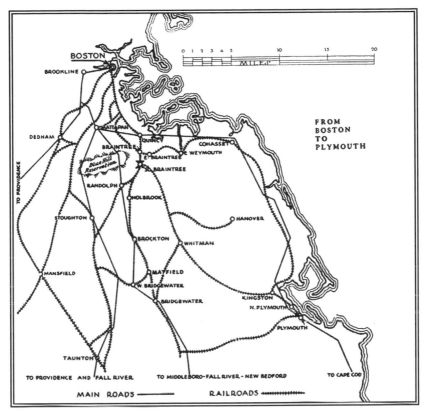

Map showing route taken by the getaway car (from the trial transcript)

Bridgewater discovered a black Buick touring car with no license plates. They notified the police. The police drove the car to headquarters in Brockton, where they searched it and learned that it had been stolen in November 1919 from Needham, not far from where the license plates had been stolen.

The discovery of the car did not help the police to advance their investigation. Although many witnesses had seen the gunmen and the shootings, their only consistent description was that they were likely foreigners. The abandoned Buick did provide one additional clue, however—on the path in the woods where it had been found, the police saw another set of tire tracks from a smaller car. This suggested that the bandits had a second vehicle, which they used after abandoning the stolen getaway car. With these bits of evidence, the police could narrow their search somewhat—they decided to look for an Italian who owned a car.

An unrelated matter advanced the investigation. Bridgewater police chief Michael Stewart two years earlier had assisted the federal Immigration Service in the arrest of six Italian anarchists who were circulating seditious literature. Under the Immigration Act of 1918, all six were scheduled for deportation, but were released on bail until they were to be deported. One of the six, Ferruccio Coacci, lived with his wife and children in West Bridgewater with another Italian immigrant, Michael Boda. Before his arrest Coacci had worked for a time at the L. Q. White factory, the Bridgewater company whose payroll was the object of the attempted holdup in December 1919. While Coacci awaited deportation, he worked for Slater & Morrill in Braintree. He had been ordered to report to the Immigration Service in Boston for deportation on April 15, 1920, but failed to show up. He called on the sixteenth to explain that he needed a few more days before reporting—his wife was sick, and he wanted to help her regain her health before he left.

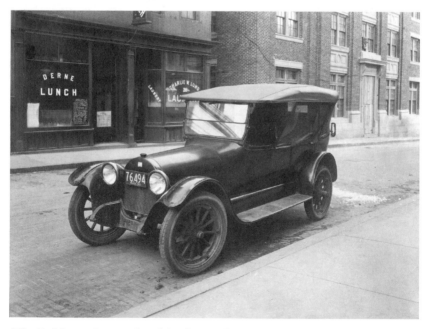

The Buick touring car found in the woods two days after the murders (courtesy of the Massachusetts Archives)

The Immigration Service called Chief Stewart and asked him to check on Coacci. Stewart sent a Bridgewater patrolman to accompany an immigration officer to visit Coacci that very evening. Coacci's wife did not seem to be ill. Coacci said he was packed and ready to leave immediately, and so the immigration officer took Coacci to Boston. The next day Coacci was transferred to New York, and on Sunday, April 18, he sailed from Ellis Island. Coacci's sudden change of heart about deportation and his wife's apparent good health puzzled Chief Stewart.

When Chief Stewart learned that the getaway car had been found less than two miles from Coacci's house, he wondered whether Coacci had been involved in the Bridgewater and Braintree crimes. He decided to go back to look around Coacci's house, which he did on Tuesday, April 20. Boda was there, and he told Chief Stewart that Mrs. Coacci and her children had moved out the day before. Stewart saw the empty garage; Boda told him his car was being repaired at Johnson's Garage, about a mile away, also in Bridgewater. After leaving, Stewart learned that Boda had also worked for the L. Q. White Company (whose payroll was the target of the failed holdup attempt in December 1919), so he decided to visit Boda again. But the next morning when Stewart knocked on Boda's door, no one answered. Stewart could see that the house was empty. Stewart thought something was amiss, but the only thing he could think to do was tell Simon Johnson, the owner of the garage where Boda left his car, to let him know when Boda came for the car.

On the evening of May 5, Boda and three other men showed up at Johnson's house, which was next door to Johnson's garage. While Johnson stalled the men, Mrs. Johnson went to a neighbor's house to call Chief Stewart. Before Stewart could get there, though, Boda and the others were gone—Boda and one man on a motorcycle, later traced through the license plate number to Ricardo Orciani, the other two on foot or on the streetcar that ran past Johnson's house to Brockton. Stewart called the Brockton police and told them to look for two foreigners on a streetcar.

Two Brockton police officers went to meet the streetcars coming in from Bridgewater. One officer boarded a trolley, saw Sacco and Vanzetti, decided they seemed like "suspicious characters," and took them to the station. When the police searched the two men they found that Vanzetti had a .38 caliber revolver, loaded with five bullets, and also had four shotgun shells. Sacco had a .32 caliber automatic pistol, fully loaded, and twenty-two loose cartridges in his pocket. Sacco also had the handwritten announcement for the upcoming rally, which was apparently to be sent to a printer. It was then that the Brockton police called Chief Stewart to tell him they had his two suspicious-looking foreigners in custody.

Stewart was not thinking of a worldwide working-class revolution; he was trying to solve the attempted Bridgewater robbery and the Braintree robbery and murders. He suspected that the robberies of the two shoe factories were related, and he surmised that they were committed by Italians who had a car. Stewart brought Simon Johnson with him to Brockton, and Johnson identified Sacco and Vanzetti as two of the men who had been at his house earlier that evening. Now, almost by chance, Stewart had in custody two Italians who, armed, had gone to pick up a car from a repair shop late at night.

Stewart found Sacco's and Vanzetti's responses to his interrogation false, evasive, and contradictory. When District Attorney Frederick Katzmann questioned Sacco and Vanzetti the next day, he asked the same questions and got the same false or evasive answers. He came to the same conclusion as Stewart—the Bridgewater attempt and the Braintree robbery and murders were committed by the same people. Katzmann decided that the five men responsible were Nicola Sacco, Bartolomeo Vanzetti, Mike Boda, Ferruccio Coacci, and Ricardo Orciani—and he set about to prosecute.

Once Katzmann determined that he had identified the culprits, it was unimportant to him that no eyewitness to either crime saw anyone as slight as the five-foot-two, one-hundred-twenty-pound Boda. (By this time, Boda was nowhere to be found, and Coacci had already been deported to Italy.) Nor was it important to him that factory time cards showed that Orciani was at work on both December 24 and April 15, and that Sacco's Three-K factory time card showed that, while he was not at work on April 15, he was on December 24. Vanzetti was the only one of the five who was in custody and without a documented alibi for either date. Katzmann theorized that Vanzetti had driven the car, despite the fact that Vanzetti did not know how to drive.

For the next several days, Katzmann brought eyewitnesses of both the Bridgewater and Braintree events to the Brockton police station to view the two prisoners. He also had witnesses in Braintree watch as he had Sacco and Vanzetti act out the shootings, basing their roles on notes police had taken from witness statements.

On June 11, based on the evidence Katzmann presented, the Plymouth County grand jury indicted Bartolomeo Vanzetti for his role in the Bridgewater robbery attempt. The Gruppo Autonomo raised nickels and dimes from the Italian community to hire lawyers and found John Vahey, a Plymouth attorney and district court judge, to represent Vanzetti as his trial opened on June 22.

The Trial

On the bench at Vanzetti's trial was Judge Webster Thayer, then sixty-two years old. Born in the small central Massachusetts town of Blackstone, he came from poor but proud Yankee stock; his father was the local butcher. Thayer attended the local public schools and then Dartmouth College, where he was an average student. After graduation he read law on his own, and was admitted to the bar in 1882. After practicing law and being politically and socially active in Worcester for thirty-five years, he was named to the Superior Court bench in 1917. An observer described Thayer as having little sympathy for foreigners, but said his fairness was beyond question.

The prosecution based its case on eyewitness identification. The payroll clerk, his guard, and two bystanders testified that Vanzetti seemed to be the man with the closely cropped mustache that they recalled seeing fire a shotgun. A woman who had seen the getaway car minutes before the robbery attempt testified that Vanzetti was the driver.

Vanzetti's lawyer should have pointed out that his client did not know how to drive. He also should have noted that it would be unlikely that the driver would also be firing a shotgun. No one seemed concerned that Vanzetti's drooping mustache did not match the witnesses' description of a closely cropped mustache on the gunman.

Judge Webster Thayer (courtesy of the Massachusetts Archives)

Vanzetti had eleven witnesses testify to his alibi for December 24. He said he had been peddling fish that day in Plymouth—delivering eels, a traditional Italian Christmas Eve dish, to his customers. All of these witnesses were members of the close-knit Italian community, and testified in Italian through a translator. The translator's poor command of English probably made their testimony less persuasive to the all-American-born jury than the testimony of prosecution witnesses, for whom English was their native tongue. On July 1 the jury found Vanzetti guilty, and Judge Thayer sentenced him to twelve to fifteen years in prison.

With Vanzetti's conviction, District Attorney Katzmann became confident he could convict Sacco and Vanzetti for the Braintree crime. On September 11, 1920, the Norfolk County grand jury indicted both men for the Braintree robbery and murders.

The Sacco and Vanzetti Defense Committee soon came together—its guiding forces were Aldino Felicani, editor of *La Notizia*, and Elizabeth Glendower Evans, a prominent Boston reformer. This alliance of Italian radicals and New England reformers was not always effective, because the disparate elements often could not agree on the best over-all strategy. The reformers saw their goal as freeing Sacco and Vanzetti, while the radicals saw their goal as overthrowing the capitalist system. But the committee did generate publicity, sending information on the trial to papers throughout the United States and Europe, and it raised money for the defense. Carlo Tresca, who had succeeded Luigi Galleani as the leader of the New York anarchists, convinced the committee to hire Fred Moore, a radical labor lawyer from California, to defend Sacco and Vanzetti. Moore had defended two IWW organizers during the 1912 Lawrence strike, and in the summer of 1920 he had success-fully defended an IWW organizer charged with dynamiting the home of a Standard Oil executive in Tulsa, Oklahoma. Moore was not famil-iar with Massachusetts rules of evidence and court procedure, so he added William Callahan, a Brockton lawyer, and Jerry McAnarney of Quincy.

Moore's strategy was to generate publicity and raise money. He spoke at meetings and persuaded local and national unions to adopt res-olutions demanding the release of Sacco and Vanzetti. He presented the two defendants as victims of a frame-up or a conspiracy. Moore and his team wrote pamphlets, weekly press releases, and articles that appeared in such magazines as *The New Republic*. At the same time, the radical and anarchist groups mobilized their followers. They organized protests and flooded the judge and prosecutor with hostile letters—Judge Thayer was receiving seven hundred per week—including many death threats. These threats only made Thayer more eager to stand up to the "Reds."

The case took an unexpected turn in late December 1920 when the Defense Committee was approached by Angelina DeFalco, an Italian interpreter in the Dedham courthouse. She told the committee that for $50,000 she could arrange acquittals for the two defendants. They should replace Moore with Percy Katzmann (District Attorney Fred Katzmann's brother). If his brother was the defense lawyer, Mrs. DeFalco said, Fred Katzmann would withdraw from the case and fix the jury.

Moore had no interest in such a scheme and arranged to have Mrs. DeFalco arrested for soliciting legal business. At her trial in January 1921, District Attorney Katzmann testified that he did not know the woman. His brother Percy Katzmann testified that he knew her because she worked as an interpreter, and said that she had tried to convince him to take over Sacco and Vanzetti's defense. But he said he knew nothing of her jury-fixing scheme. The judge in the case said Mrs. DeFalco had acted unwisely, but was innocent of any crime. More important, he cleared the Katzmanns of any wrongdoing.

District Attorney Fred Katzmann regarded the DeFalco affair as an attack on his personal integrity. His prosecution of Sacco and Vanzetti had languished until this episode. In fact, Katzmann had not been eager to move ahead to trial since his investigators had not developed any significant new evidence. Now this personal element made Katzmann press his prosecution team to work on the case with new energy.

SECURITY WAS TIGHT AROUND THE Dedham courthouse as the trial opened on Tuesday, May 31, 1921. The courthouse was guarded against possible attack. State police, rifles at the ready, patrolled outside, and everyone entering the building was searched for weapons.

Selecting a jury was tedious. Moore excluded any prospective juror he thought was too educated, believing that his working-class clients would be best served by men who identified with their status. It took four full days to select the jury.

On Monday, June 6, the members of the jury were taken to the scene of the crime, Johnson's house and garage, and the woods where the getaway car was discovered. The next day, Assistant District Attorney Harold Williams began the prosecution's case by outlining all the evidence the prosecution intended to introduce. For the next nineteen days Katzmann would seek to prove that Sacco and Vanzetti had murdered Parmenter and Berardelli. He based his case on five main categories of evidence: eyewitnesses who could identify Sacco and Vanzetti and place them at the scene of the crime; expert testimony that the bullet that had killed Berardelli came from Sacco's gun; proof that when he was arrested, Vanzetti had Berardelli's gun; that the cap found on Pearl Street after the shootings belonged to Sacco; and the "consciousness of guilt" Vanzetti and Sacco displayed when arrested.

The first series of witnesses were those who claimed to have witnessed the shooting. Mark Carrigan said that the getaway car drove right past him. A man with a gun "had black hair. It was kind of long . . . He looked, possibly, like an Italian." Jimmy Bostock, a mechanic at Slater & Morrill, had been on the street and had actually spoken to Parmenter a few moments before the shooting started. They discussed a machine that needed some repair, and then Bostock continued to walk down the street. When he heard shots, he turned to see a gunman, wearing a cap, firing at Berardelli. Bostock took a step toward Berardelli when the guard fell, but stopped in his tracks when the gunman fired at him. Bostock saw the third robber get out of the car to help load the money boxes, and then watched as the car drove right past him. He had taken the dying Berardelli in his arms. The prosecutor asked Bostock whether he could say that the defendants were the robbers he saw. Bostock answered, "No sir. I could not tell whether they was, no sir."

Several days after the shooting, Bostock had been shown a collection of mug shots. He had picked out a photograph of Anthony Palmisano, a New York bank robber, as one of the gunmen. A week later, taking a second look at mug shots, he again picked out Palmisano. When Bostock came to the Brockton police station the day after Sacco and Vanzetti were arrested, he said that he did not think either of these men was the gunman.

Several witnesses in nearby buildings said they had looked out their windows when they heard shots. Other witnesses said they had seen one or the other of the defendants earlier in the day, or in the car during the getaway. Though several witnesses identified Sacco as the gunman who shot Berardelli, other witnesses insisted Sacco was not that gunman. No witness had seen the other gunman fire a shot, and no witness identified Vanzetti as the other robber.

JAMES MCGLONE WAS EXCAVATING a foundation for a building directly across from the Rice & Hutchins factory, about twenty feet from the shooting. He saw a gunman hold Berardelli by the shoulder and shoot him twice. He testified that he could not say that either defendant was this gunman.

The eyewitnesses had trouble linking either Sacco or Vanzetti to the crime scene until Lola Andrews took the stand. Lola Andrews, a divorced woman who occasionally worked as a nurse, testified that she and a friend, the elderly Mrs. Julia Campbell, had gone to South Braintree on the morning of April 15 to look for work. At about 11:30 A.M., as the two women walked to the Slater & Morrill factory, she saw a man working under a car, as if trying to fix it, and another man standing next to the car. The men were still there a few minutes later, when Andrews and Campbell left the factory. Mrs. Andrews described the man standing by the car as "light skinned and sickly looking." Mrs. Andrews said she asked the man working under the car how to find the entrance to the Rice & Hutchins factory. She testified that he slid out from under the car, stood up, and pointed the way. This allowed her to get a closer look at him, and she described him as dark skinned and wearing dark clothes. When she was brought to the Dedham jail in February 1921, she had looked at a number of prisoners and identified Sacco as the man who had given her the directions.

The defense did not ask Mrs. Andrews why she had asked for directions from the man under the car, rather than the man standing beside it. Mrs. Andrews told a slightly different story upon cross-examination, however. She said that she had not picked Sacco out at the Dedham jail, saying that District Attorney Katzmann had pressured her to say that Sacco was the man under the car. Mrs. Andrews's companion, Mrs. Campbell, testified that they did not stop to talk to the man working under the car. When Moore interviewed Mrs. Andrews before the trial, he showed her photographs of Sacco, and she told him that the man in the photographs was not the man under the car.

Prosecution witness Lewis Pelser, a worker in the Rice & Hutchins factory, said he was working on the first floor of the factory when he heard three shots fired outside. He opened the window in time to see a gunman fire a fourth shot into Berardelli, just ten feet from the window. He said he saw the gunman fire another shot toward Parmenter, then run toward the getaway car. As the gunman fired several shots toward the building, Pelser was able to record the car's license number. Asked if Sacco was the gunman, Pelser testified: "I wouldn't say he is the man, but he is the dead image of the man I seen."

Pelser had told the police a somewhat different story after the defendants had been arrested. At that time he said he had not seen enough of the robbery to be able to identify anyone. When a defense investigator interviewed Pelser in advance of the trial, Pelser again said that he had not seen the shooting. Pelser retracted the statement under cross-examination, saying he had lied to the investigator because he did not want to have to testify. Three of Pelser's coworkers testified that they and Pelser had all ducked under a bench when they heard the shooting, and no one looked out the window.

Barbara Liscomb also worked on the first floor of the Rice & Hutchins factory. When she heard the shooting on April 15 she had looked out another first-floor window. She testified that she saw a gunman standing over Berardelli. The gunman looked right at her, giving her a good look at his face. Sacco was not that man.

The very last prosecution witness to the shooting was Victrola salesman Carlos Goodridge. He testified that he had been in a poolroom just down the street from the crime scene, and that he had stepped out of the poolroom when he heard the shots. The getaway car "was coming towards me possibly at a rate of ten or twelve miles an hour." A man leaned out of the car, "a dark-complexioned fellow, with dark hair," and pointed a gun at him, "a dark-colored revolver, shining barrel to it." He said the man was Sacco. The defense knew that Goodridge was actually a petty thief who had pleaded guilty to a charge of larceny in the Dedham court in September 1920. The defense suggested that Goodridge had been given a suspended sentence in exchange for his

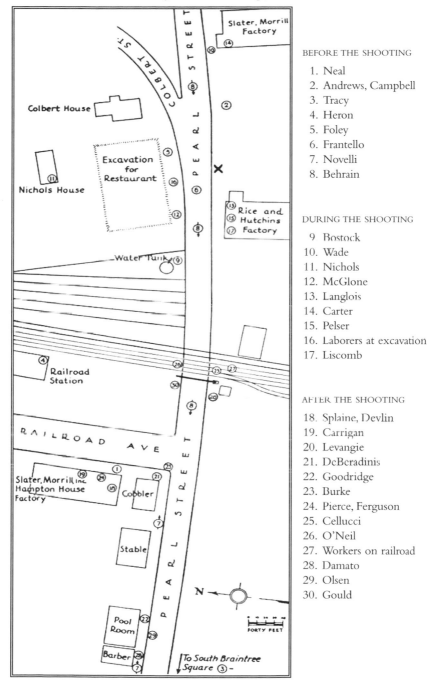

THE NEIGHBORHOOD OF THE CRIME
(from the trial transcript)

BEFORE THE SHOOTING

1. Neal
2. Andrews, Campbell
3. Tracy
4. Heron
5. Foley
6. Frantello
7. Novelli
8. Behrain

DURING THE SHOOTING

9. Bostock
10. Wade
11. Nichols
12. McGlone
13. Langlois
14. Carter
15. Pelser
16. Laborers at excavation
17. Liscomb

AFTER THE SHOOTING

18. Splaine, Devlin
19. Carrigan
20. Levangie
21. DeBeradinis
22. Goodridge
23. Burke
24. Pierce, Ferguson
25. Cellucci
26. O'Neil
27. Workers on railroad
28. Damato
29. Olsen
30. Gould

testimony against Sacco. Judge Thayer would not allow the defense to make any reference to Goodridge's criminal record or this suggestion of leniency.

Having done his best to place Sacco at the scene, Katzmann next introduced witnesses against Vanzetti. Pattern maker John Faulkner testified that on the morning of the murder he had ridden the 9:20 train from Plymouth to Boston. He said on the morning of April 15 a man had sat next to him and at each station asked if they were at East Braintree yet. Asked to describe the man's appearance, Faulkner testified, "Why, he looked like a foreigner, with a black mustache and cheekbones. He had a felt hat on, kind of old clothes." The man finally got off when the train reached East Braintree. In July 1920 the district attorney brought Faulkner to the jail, where he picked Vanzetti out of a lineup of five men. The defense showed that on April 15, the day of the crime, no one had bought a cash ticket to East Braintree either at a station or on the train. Under cross-examination, Faulkner admitted that after the arrest he had seen Vanzetti's picture in the newspaper. Moore suggested that Faulkner's identification was colored by having seen the photographs.

Harry Dolbeare, a piano tuner, testified that at around ten in the morning he had noticed five men sitting in a car in South Braintree Square. Asked why he had noticed them, he testified, "They appeared strange to me, as strangers to the town, as a carload of foreigners ... I felt it was a tough-looking bunch." He said Bartolomeo Vanzetti was one of the three men in the back seat of that car.

WITH UNRELIABLE AND CONTRADICTORY witnesses, the prosecution would rely on ballistic evidence connecting Sacco's gun with the bullets found in the murdered men. Ballistic evidence is based on the fact that each gun barrel makes a distinctive set of marks on bullets as they are fired. Gun barrels have spirals cut into them to make the bullet spin, giving it greater speed and accuracy. These spirals will leave scratches on the bullet, and no two guns will make the precise same marks on a bullet. An expert examining a bullet under a microscope can determine whether a particular gun fired a particular bullet.

Dr. George Magrath, the medical examiner who had removed the four bullets from Berardelli's body, described where he had found each bullet and explained how he had scratched a Roman numeral on each one with a surgical needle. He determined that the third, on which he had scratched the Roman numeral III, was the fatal bullet. This bullet had passed through Berardelli's chest and lodged in his abdomen. During the trial's third week, on June 18, 1921, ballistics tests were conducted using Sacco's gun. State police captain William Proctor represented the prosecution, along with Charles Van Amburgh, who worked for the Remington Company, an ammunition manufacturer. Representing Sacco and Vanzetti was James Burns, an engineer employed by the U.S. Cartridge Company, another ammunition manufacturer. These experts fired a total of twenty bullets through Sacco's gun and then compared the markings on these bullets with Bullet III.

The guns Sacco and Vanzetti were carrying when they were arrested, along with the bullets removed from the bodies of Parmenter and Berardelli, the spent shells found on the street, and several bullets Vanzetti was carrying when he was arrested (courtesy of the Massachusetts Archives)

Captain Proctor testified that five of the bullets removed from the two murdered men (Berardelli had been shot four times, Parmenter twice) had right-hand spiral markings, and one, Bullet III, had left-hand spirals. Colt automatics, such as Sacco's gun, always leave left-hand spirals. Therefore, Sacco's gun could not have fired five of the six bullets, but could have fired the fatal Bullet III. The ballistics experts compared Bullet III with test bullets fired from Sacco's pistol to determine if in fact the gun had shot the bullet that killed Berardelli.

The evidence about Bullet III was ambiguous. Proctor, a state police captain for sixteen years, had been involved in the initial investigations in Bridgewater and Braintree, and had testified as an expert in over one hundred capital cases. Before he appeared in court, Captain Proctor told Katzmann that the markings did not convince him that the bullet was fired by Sacco's gun. So, when Katzmann called on Proctor to testify about Bullet III, he carefully worded his question: "Have you an opinion as to whether Bullet III was fired from [Sacco's pistol]?" Proctor did have an opinion, he said, and he was also careful in choosing his words: "My opinion is that it is consistent with being fired from that pistol." For some reason, the defense did not follow up on this rather vague statement.

Two years later, when the defense was seeking a new trial, Proctor submitted an affidavit explaining his doubts in more detail. He said that he had told the prosecutor that if he were asked in court whether he thought the tests proved that Sacco's gun had fired the bullet, he would have answered in the negative. Katzmann knew that Proctor's testimony was crucial, so he badgered Proctor to make his denial more equivocal. In his 1923 affidavit Proctor said, "If they had asked me any more particularly than that I should have told them I didn't think it went through that gun and I did tell the District Attorney before the trial I thought it was consistent with going through that type of gun, but I don't think it went through that gun."

Charles Van Amburgh said that the scratches on the test bullets were similar to the scratches on Bullet III. When asked his opinion about Bullet III, he testified, "I am inclined to believe it was fired from [the Sacco] pistol." Van Amburgh's statement that he was "inclined to believe" the bullet came from Sacco's gun should have been an opening for the defense to challenge him on cross-examination, but the defense made no such challenge.

James Burns, the defense's ballistics expert, looked at the same markings on Bullet III but reached the opposite conclusion from Van Amburgh. After he compared the measurements of the markings on Bullet III to those on eleven test bullets, he was the most certain of the three expert witnesses. Asked if he thought Bullet III had been fired from Sacco's gun, he testified, "Not in my opinion, no."

In addition to maintaining that Bullet III was not fired from Sacco's gun, Sacco and Vanzetti's defenders also argued that Bullet III was not even the same bullet that Dr. Magrath had removed from Berardelli's body. At some point, the defense later claimed, someone had switched the evidence, replacing the real fatal bullet with one to incriminate Nicola Sacco.

All of the eyewitnesses to the shootings said that one gunman had done all the shooting. Not a single witness testified that the other gunman had fired a shot, and no one said that the first gunman used two guns. It seems strange that six bullets were recovered from Parmenter and Berardelli's bodies, and five of them had identical markings but one—the fatal bullet—did not. All three ballistics experts agreed that Bullet III did not come from the same gun as the other five bullets removed from the two dead men. Where did Bullet III come from? Careful comparison of the numerals scratched on the bullets suggested that the marks on Bullet III were made by a needle less sharp than the one that made the marks on Bullets I, II, and IV, and by a person with a clumsier hand.

WHEN MAGRATH REMOVED THE FOUR bullets from Berardelli's body, he put each one in an envelope and gave those envelopes to Captain Proctor. There was no formal record of the custody of the bullets from the day Proctor received them until they were presented at the trial and introduced as exhibits. Even during the trial, the bullets were handled by a number of witnesses and court personnel, and there was no apparent effort made to maintain any control over the custody of the bullets.

There were also several spent shells in evidence. Shortly after the shooting, James Bostock picked up three or four shells on the street and turned them over to Thomas Fraher, Slater & Morrill's plant superintendent, who a day later gave them to Captain Proctor. These shells were later referred to as the "Fraher shells."

Katzmann had told Moore before the trial started that he did not intend to argue that any particular bullet had come from any particular gun. But after the ballistics tests on June 18, three weeks into the trial, he told Moore that he withdrew that statement. Long after the trial, when the lawyers were trying to get a new trial for Sacco and Vanzetti, the defense developed a theory that at the ballistics test someone had replaced the original Bullet III with a bullet fired by Sacco's gun.

The proponents of the "switched bullet" theory argued that Katzmann had known before the trial that none of the bullets removed from the two bodies had been fired by a Colt revolver, which is why he told Moore that he would not present any evidence connecting any bullet to either gun. However, after the ballistics test, when he had a bullet that had been fired from a Colt, he withdrew his earlier stipulation. The unfortunate part of this theory, from the point of view of the defense, was that it was in effect an allegation of fraud on the part of the prosecution, and they had no evidence to support such a claim. Though no witnesses saw the second gunman fire a shot, Vanzetti was also carrying a gun—a fully loaded nickel-plated .38 caliber Harrington & Richardson revolver—when he was arrested on the streetcar on May 5. The prosecution claimed that this was Berardelli's gun, that Sacco had taken it from the fallen Berardelli after he shot him, and had given it to Vanzetti. Vanzetti claimed that he had bought the gun from a dealer several years earlier, although he did not remember the name of the dealer. Since the gun's serial number could not be traced to any store from which either Berardelli or Vanzetti might have bought it, proof of ownership would have to be based on other evidence.

Sarah Berardelli, Allesandro's widow, testified that her husband usually carried a gun, and this revolver looked like the gun he owned. She testified that on March 20, 1920, she had accompanied her husband to a gun shop in Boston to have a broken spring repaired. She did not know whether Allesandro had gotten this particular gun back from the repair shop before the murder, but she did know that in early April he had a gun. A repair shop employee testified that they had received a .38 caliber Harrington & Richardson revolver from Berardelli. Another gun shop employee examined the disputed .38 caliber revolver in the courtroom and said that it appeared to have a new hammer, not a new spring. He also testified that, while the repair shop had no record of Berardelli picking up the gun, the gun was not in the shop nor had it been sold, as unclaimed guns sometimes were.

The day after he was arrested, Vanzetti had told Katzmann that he carried the gun to protect his fish cart. He said that he had bought the gun in Boston four or five years earlier—although he could not remember where—and had paid eighteen or nineteen dollars for it. Now in court he testified that he had actually bought the gun several months earlier from fellow anarchist Luigi Falzini for five dollars. He admitted in court that he had lied to Katzmann at the time of his arrest to protect his anarchist friends. The defense brought in a series of witnesses to establish this chain of ownership, starting with a man from Maine who said that he recognized the gun (from the scratches on the barrel) as one he had bought years earlier from his mother-in-law. He later sold the gun to coworker, Ricardo Orciani. Falzini testified that he had bought the gun from Orciani and sold it to Vanzetti.

While the testimony about the bullets and the gun was inconclusive, the prosecution did have one piece of tangible evidence that they said proved Sacco was the gunman—a gray cloth cap found on the street near where Berardelli's body had fallen. Fred Loring, a Slater & Morrill employee, testified that he picked up this cap some time after the shooting, as people were milling about the scene. He turned it over to plant superintendent Thomas Fraher, who turned it over to the police the next day. A Pinkerton detective working on the case noted that the hat was "a heavy winter cap about 6 $7/8$ size." The prosecution argued that this was Sacco's cap, which had fallen off his head during the shooting. The cap had no identification on it, but it did have a tear in the lining. The issue was whether the prosecution could prove that the hat was indeed Sacco's.

George Kelley, the superintendent at the Three-K shoe plant, testified that Sacco ordinarily wore a hat similar to the one the prosecution was presenting as evidence. The prosecution pressed Kelley hard to identify the hat as Sacco's. He would say only that the hat was "similar in color" to the cap Sacco usually wore, and similar "in general appearance" to Sacco's usual caps. He said that another cap, which the police had seized in Sacco's house, was more like what he remembered Sacco wearing.

Kelley also said that Sacco usually hung his cap on a nail or a wooden peg in the factory. The prosecution suggested that the hole in the lining might have been caused by hanging the hat repeatedly on a nail. Years later, Braintree police chief Jeremiah Gallivan told the Lowell Committee he had torn the hole in the cap to find identification.

District Attorney Katzmann asked Sacco to try on the hat. Sacco put it on his head. He said it was too tight, but Katzmann said it seemed to fit fine. Sacco also said that the disputed cap had earflaps, and he never bought a cap with earflaps. Sacco was also asked to try on the cap that the police had seized in his house the day after he was arrested. That cap, size 7 1/8, fitted perfectly.

WHILE THE PHYSICAL EVIDENCE was ambiguous at best, the prosecution's real case was built on Sacco and Vanzetti's "consciousness of guilt." Katzmann argued that their actions and statements at the time of their arrest were not consistent with innocence, and Judge Thayer later described these deeds and words as demonstrating "consciousness of guilt." One key issue: Why had the defendants been so nervous at the Johnson house?

The fact that they had watched Mrs. Johnson so carefully when she went to the neighbor's house was presented as evidence of their consciousness of guilt. According to the prosecution, the four men left the Johnsons' house abruptly when they noticed telephone wires running from the neighbor's house (not every house had a telephone in 1920). According to the defense, there was an innocent reason for them to leave—when Johnson asked Boda if he had a 1920 license plate and Boda said he did not, Johnson told him it would not be wise to drive the car.

When Sacco and Vanzetti were arrested, Chief Stewart questioned them about why they had gone to the Johnson house, why they were carrying guns, and about their political beliefs and activities. He did not tell them that they were suspects in either the Bridgewater or the Braintree case.

Both men lied to him at the time of their arrest to protect themselves and their anarchist friends. They had been warned a few days earlier that another round of "Palmer raids" was likely, and they wanted to collect subversive literature and hide it from the authorities until the danger passed. They had legitimate fear for their own safety. Just two days earlier, their friend Andrea Salsedo had died while in custody after falling from a fourteenth-story window in a federal office building in New York. Whether he jumped or was pushed was never determined.

They denied knowing Boda and Orciani, they denied having been at the Johnson house, and they said they had not seen anyone on a motorcycle. The prosecution drew a logical inference from these "obvious lies": Sacco and Vanzetti were conscious of their guilt.

The prosecution finally rested its case on June 21, 1921, the nineteenth day of the trial. William Callahan made the opening statement for Sacco, saying the defense would present two groups of witnesses: those who would contradict the prosecution's witnesses about the gunmen's identity, and those who had seen the defendants elsewhere at the time of the shootings. Callahan said the defendants themselves would also testify.

The defense produced more than a dozen eyewitnesses who had seen the shooting or been near the scene, and could say that neither Sacco nor Vanzetti was a gunman. Frank Burke, a glassblower, testified that he was walking on the street as the two gunmen ran toward him and jumped into the moving getaway car. Albert Frantello, a former Slater & Morrill employee, was walking on the sidewalk past the two men leaning against the fence—the two men who moments later were the gunmen. Frantello said he had gotten a good look at both of them, and neither was Sacco or Vanzetti. Five laborers who had been digging an excavation across Pearl Street testified that they saw the shooting or saw the getaway car pick up the gunmen. All five testified that neither Sacco nor Vanzetti was a gunman. Several pedestrians who had seen the gunmen standing around on the street before the shooting, two shoe company workers who had watched the robbery from a factory window, and several witnesses who had seen the gunmen drive off testified that neither Sacco nor Vanzetti was there. Mrs. Julia Campbell contradicted her friend Lola Andrews, with whom she had been walking that morning. Mrs. Campbell said that they had asked a man working under a car for directions, but the man they asked was not Nicola Sacco.

The defense then called witnesses to prove that Sacco and Vanzetti were somewhere else at the time of the crime. Sacco's alibi was that he was in Boston all day on April 15. He had taken the train to Boston early that morning to get passports for himself and his family at the Italian consulate. Witnesses remembered talking with Nicola Sacco in Boston on April 15. Felice Guadagni, a professor of literature and editor of an Italian language newspaper, testified that he had lunch with Sacco in a particular restaurant and described their conversation. Albert Bosco, editor for another Italian language paper, was also present at this lunch. Katzmann, on cross-examination, asked both men how they could recall so certainly that the day was Thursday, April 15, and not any other particular day. They recalled because the subject of their conversation was a banquet an Italian civic group was hosting that evening, April 15, honoring John Williams, editor of the *Boston Transcript*.

Giuseppe Andrower, a consulate official, testified by deposition (he had been transferred back to Italy in May 1920). He remembered that on April 15 Sacco, seeking passports for himself, Rosina, and Dante, had come to the consulate with an enormous family portrait. Andrower recalled the date and the incident because it had been a relatively quiet day in the consulate, and he found Sacco's story so amusing that he had told the consul about it.

Vanzetti's alibi for April 15 was that he was in Plymouth all that day. Katzmann tried to shake the witnesses who remembered seeing Vanzetti on April 15—how could they be so sure of that particular date? Why not some other date? He would ask about random dates, or other events, in an often successful attempt to confuse the witnesses. For example, Angel Guidobone, a rug worker, remembered getting his weekly codfish from Vanzetti shortly after noon on April 15. He had paid for it the day before, and remembered the transaction because on Monday the nineteenth he went into the hospital with appendicitis.

"I bought it on the fourteenth, and on the fifteenth I got the fish in my hand, and I had it." Katzmann asked if Guidobone could have "bought the fish on the thirteenth and been operated on on the nineteenth?" Guidobone asked if Katzmann "want me to buy fish months before and then eat it months afterward?" No, but Katzmann asked if the thirteenth was "months before" the nineteenth? "Why, no, but do you think I keep a fish in the house for a week?"

Katzmann asked why Guidobone was so sure he'd bought the fish on the fourteenth, and not on the twelfth or thirteenth? "Well, of course, I remember I had the pain here on the nineteenth and I went and had the operation, and of course I got the cut here, and then I know." Katzmann took Guidobone's word for the operation—of course he would remember that—but how would he remember buying fish on April fourteenth?

"Well," Guidobone answered, "how could I say today is Thursday and could I say it is Wednesday?"

"Well," Katzmann responded, "how can you say it was the fifteenth and not the thirteenth; the fish was put right in your hand and you had it?"

"Because it was not so. Because it was not so." Guidobone was sure he had the fish in his hand on Thursday, April 15—as he had every Thursday before that, but not the Thursday afterward—because he bought fish every Thursday to eat on Friday. He did not remember the date, but he knew the days of the week. On Fridays Catholics abstained from eating meat, so would naturally buy fish. Guidobone had bought fish from Vanzetti every Thursday, but would not have bought it the week after his operation. Melvin Corl, a fisherman, remembered talking with Vanzetti for an hour and a half on April 15. He remembered because he was not fishing that day, but had spent the week painting his boat, which he hoped to get in the water the next day. He did not, but got the boat in the water on Saturday, April 17.

"Does that date mean anything to you?" Katzmann asked.

"It was my wife's birthday."

The peddler Joseph Rosen remembered selling Vanzetti a piece of cloth, with a hole in it, on April 15. Vanzetti had brought the cloth to Alphonsine Brini to inspect, and she also testified that Vanzetti had come home with the cloth that afternoon. Rosen had also sold cloth that day to the Plymouth police chief's wife, but she was not called, and could not verify that Rosen had sold cloth to Vanzetti.

Moore realized he had a problem with all these defense witnesses: All were either Italians or Jews. He knew he could produce more witnesses who had spoken with Vanzetti or Sacco on April 15, but all were Italians, and the jurors, all Yankees, would grow disgusted and believe that all Italians were synchronizing their testimony. Katzmann had ridiculed the peddler Rosen, and discounted all the testimony of the Italians of Plymouth and Boston.

Vanzetti had not taken the stand in his first trial, but he did at his second, on July 5, 1921. Defense attorney Jerry McAnarney carefully led him through his life story, beginning with his youth in Italy, his arrival in the United States in 1908, and his life in America up until April 15, 1920. The first reference in the trial to the anarchist backgrounds of the two defendants was made when McAnarney asked Vanzetti why he had gone to the Johnson house on May 5. Vanzetti described his radical activities, his trip to New York to learn about Salsedo's fate, and his plan to collect and hide anarchist materials. He said they wanted to go to their friends' houses because they feared the police might "go there and take letters and take books and take newspapers and put men in jail and deport [them]."

On cross-examination, Katzmann focused on the lies Vanzetti had told when Stewart and Katzmann questioned him shortly after the arrest. Katzmann's premise was that the lies revealed the defendants' "consciousness of guilt" about the shootings. He tried to show that the defendants' purported reasons for lying—fear of deportation for their radical activities, or fear of arrest for dodging the draft—were hardly adequate to explain their behavior. Some of those lies were consistent with Vanzetti's stated purpose—to avoid identifying other radicals. However, several of the lies were quite damaging. Vanzetti had originally told Katzmann that he had bought his gun at a shop in Boston years earlier for eighteen or nineteen dollars. Now, in court, he testified that he had bought it just a few months earlier, from Falzini, for five dollars. Judge Thayer later (in rejecting one of the motions for a new trial) observed that if Vanzetti really did not know the gun's market value, the jury could have surmised that he had not bought it. Rather, as the prosecution claimed, he had taken it from Berardelli.

Katzmann also explored Sacco and Vanzetti's 1917 Mexican trip. He approached the subject as part of his "consciousness of guilt" line of questioning. He got Vanzetti to admit that, as an alien, he was not subject to being drafted, so his alleged concern about being arrested for draft dodging was not credible. This line of inquiry also prejudiced the patriotic jurors against Vanzetti and Sacco.

Sacco testified more directly than Vanzetti had about the anarchist movement, Salsedo's death, and the reason for collecting the radical literature. Katzmann's cross-examination, however, was devastating. Sacco had said the reason for his coming to the United States was his love "for a free country." Katzmann used that statement as the basis for a series of inflammatory questions, challenging how Sacco could he say he loved the United States when he ran away from military service in the war. A short sample of Katzmann's questions, as recorded in the trial transcript, illustrates the point:

"Did you love this country in May 1917?"

"In order to show your love for the United States of America when she was about to call on you to become a soldier, you ran away to Mexico?"

"Did you go to Mexico to avoid being a soldier for this country that you loved?"

"Would it be your idea of showing your love for your wife that when she needed you, you ran away from her?"

"Did you love your country when you came back from Mexico?"

Sacco said the main reason he came back from Mexico was that he could not earn enough money to survive. Katzmann asked a series of questions about how much money Sacco had made when he first came to the United States and worked as a laborer, and then later as he became a skilled factory worker. When Sacco explained how he had progressed from $1.15 per day as a laborer to more than $50 per week in the shoe factory, Katzmann returned to the subject of how little money Sacco was able to earn in Mexico. Then Katzmann continued the attack:

"Is your love for the United States of America commensurate with the amount of money you can get in this country in a week?"

"Is the extent of your love for this country measured in dollars and cents?"

"Is your love for this country measured by the amount of money you can earn here?"

The cross-examination continued to explore other reasons Sacco was not happy in Mexico and returned to the United States—such reasons as the strange language, the unavailability of Italian food, and his longing to be with his wife and son. At every opportunity, Katzmann used the exchange to mock Sacco's statement about his love for the United States.

McAnarney objected to the entire line of the cross-examination. Judge Thayer used that objection as an opportunity to begin an extraordinary exercise in cross-examination himself. Although he addressed his questions to McAnarney, the effect was to continue the cross-examination of Sacco. He asked McAnarney a series of questions, and six times the judge asked:

"Are you going to claim that the collection of the literature and the books was really in the interest of the United States?"

McAnarney said that he was making no such claim, and objected that the question was prejudicial to the defendants. Judge Thayer responded by repeating the question a seventh time. He then said Katzmann could resume his cross-examination since the witness was not going to argue that he was benefiting the United States in some way by collecting the anarchist literature.

Katzmann continued to press Sacco on his professed love for the United States, and invited him to explain just what he meant. Sacco rose to the bait and began a lengthy and emotional speech. He described his hopes when he first came to this country, about how hard he worked and how little money he made, how he saw the injustice of the capitalist system, the imprisonment of leading socialists for their beliefs, the burdens of the working poor, the lack of opportunity for advancement (he used Harvard College as an example of an unattainable goal for the youth of working-class families), his feeling that war

Editorial cartoon in the **Boston Post,** *1921, during the trial (courtesy of the Massachusetts Archives)*

benefited no one but big business—all of which justified his objective of destroying all governments.

When Sacco finished, emotionally and physically drained, Katzmann calmly resumed his cross-examination, and challenged each of the points Sacco had made. McAnarney objected to the continued prejudice and irrelevance of this line of questioning. Judge Thayer over-ruled him, saying that Katzmann was merely addressing points Sacco had initially raised.

After a few more witnesses were called to corroborate or rebut minor points from earlier in the trial, both sides rested their cases and the lawyers began their closing arguments. Each side presented four hours of closing arguments—summarizing the evidence they thought supported their side, pointing out the defects in the evidence that did not. Moore focused on the weaknesses in the testimony of Lola Andrews and Richard Pelser, since they were key witnesses placing Sacco at the scene. McAnarney reiterated the pressure that Goodridge was under to testify for the prosecution. Katzmann made a similar effort to belittle the testimony of defense witnesses, and to buttress the testi-mony of the prosecution witnesses. For example, he said that in his long years of service, he could not recall "so convincing a witness as Lola Andrews." Then Judge Thayer presented his charge to the jury. He explained the legal definition of murder, and the manner in which the jury was to evaluate the evidence they had heard. He specifically instructed the jury not to be prejudiced against the defendants because they were Italians, but he also referred several times to the jurors' loy-alty to America, to their citizenship, praising each juror as someone who "is loyal to God, to country, to his state and to his fellow men, repre-sents the highest and noblest type of true American citizenship . . . ." The jurors deliberated for less than three hours. They found both Sacco and Vanzetti guilty of two counts of murder in the first degree.

CHAPTER FOUR

Motions for a New Trial

T he jury's verdict on July 14, 1921, was not the end of the case. Over the next two years, defense counsel would file seven separate motions for a new trial. Under Massachusetts law at the time, the original trial judge would hear any motion for a new trial. So Judge Webster Thayer would consider each of the defense's arguments that he had not given Sacco and Vanzetti a fair trial.

The first motion asked Thayer to overturn the jury's verdict on the grounds that it was against the weight of the evidence. This is a standard posttrial motion in a murder case. Judge Thayer said that he was not allowed to overturn the jury unless he found that they were manifestly mistaken in their assessment of the evidence or that, because of prejudice against the defendants, they had violated their oaths as jurors. This motion was argued in court on October 29, 1921.

Fred Moore argued that eyewitness testimony was insufficient. Several witnesses put Sacco at the scene of the crime, but just as many said Sacco was not the gunman, and not one eyewitness had seen Vanzetti. More important, the jury had not given proper weight to the defense's alibis, witnesses who testified that both defendants were elsewhere at the time of the shootings. Katzmann supported the jury's verdict, describing the eye-witnesses who identified Sacco as one of the robbers. Sacco interrupted

Katzmann's presentation several times, saying that Katzmann had told the witnesses to identify him. Vanzetti shouted that Katzmann had brought every crook in Massachusetts to testify against them.

In his written decision of December 24, 1921, denying the motion to overturn the jury's verdict, Judge Thayer said that there was ample evidence to convict Sacco and Vanzetti other than eyewitness testimony. He summarized the ballistic evidence, the fatal bullet and Sacco's gun, the cap found on the ground near Berardelli's body, the weakness of the defendants' alibis, and the consciousness of guilt—the lies the defendants had told when they were first questioned by Chief Stewart and District Attorney Katzmann. The testimony could "overwhelmingly and irresistibly" convince the jury to reach its guilty verdicts. As to Moore's argument that the jurors were prejudiced against the defendants because they were foreigners, anarchists, and draft dodgers, Thayer said that the members of the jury had been subjected to rigorous examination before being seated, that they had been sequestered throughout the trial, and he had not, until the motion was argued, heard any suggestion of prejudice.

The defense filed five more motions between November 1921 and April 1923, each one based on new evidence that might justify reopening the case. Judge Thayer heard arguments over these motions two years later in late October and early November 1923.

The Ripley Motion

The first of these motions resulted from a conversation between defense counsel Jerry McAnarney and jury foreman Walter Ripley a month after the trial. Ripley told McAnarney that he had brought three bullets from home into the jury room so that the jurors could look at them, and that the jurors had compared these bullets to those taken from Vanzetti's gun. The defense argued that it was improper for the jury to consider evidence that is not a regular exhibit in the case. Since Ripley had died shortly after relating his story to McAnarney, it could not be determined why he had brought these bullets into the jury room. But a few days before Judge Thayer heard arguments on this motion, defense counsel learned of a conversation Ripley had had with

a neighbor, William Daly, during the last week o[...]
days before the trial started. Daly reported that Ri[...]
he was going to be a juror in the trial of "the[...]
Guineas," referring to Sacco and Vanzetti. When I[...]
made sense that someone who had worked at tha[...]
rob its payroll in broad daylight, Ripley replied[...]
ought to hang anyway." The defense filed Daly's affidavit as a supple-
ment to the Ripley motion, arguing that even before the trial, Ripley
had formed an opinion about the defendants' guilt. Moore argued that
since the foreman of the jury was biased, and he might use his position
of authority to sway the jurors, this certainly justified a new trial.

Judge Thayer dismissed the argument that the jurors might have
been improperly influenced by comparing Ripley's bullets with the
alleged Vanzetti bullets. The judge discussed at great length the fact that
three weeks had passed between Vanzetti's testimony about the bullets
and Ripley's presentation of his bullets. Thayer thought it unlikely that
by examining Ripley's bullets the jurors would discern any discrepancy
between these bullets and Vanzetti's testimony. As to any statement
Ripley might have made to Daly, the judge could not consider it as evidence because Ripley was dead, and the story could not be verified.

The Gould Motion

Several more defense motions argued against the credibility of
prosecution witnesses, or introduced new witnesses whom the court
had overlooked. Traveling salesman Roy Gould had been crossing Pearl
Street a block from the scene of the robbery. Someone in the getaway
car fired at him as it passed, at a distance of no more than ten feet, sending a bullet through his overcoat. In describing the gunman to a policeman, Gould said he would never forget his face. The description—a
man about twenty-two to twenty-five years old, of slight build—did
not fit either Sacco or Vanzetti. The police took down Gould's address,
but he was not called as a witness, and the prosecution did not tell the
defense about Gould or his statement.

After the trial, the defense interviewed Gould. He signed an affidavit
summarizing what he had told the policeman at the scene. Moore took

see Sacco in jail in November 1921, and had him study pho-
os of Vanzetti. Gould said that neither Sacco nor Vanzetti was the
n who had shot at him. Moore argued that the prosecution had con-
cealed this witness whose story conflicted with the prosecution's theory
of the case.

Judge Thayer dismissed this motion, ruling that Gould was simply
one more eyewitness, and there had been a large number of eyewitnesses with conflicting stories. Since the verdict rested more on the
physical evidence and the defendants' consciousness of guilt, Thayer said
Gould's testimony would not have altered the verdict. Thayer also noted
that Gould had not seen Sacco between April 15, 1920, and November
10, 1921, so his affidavit now claimed that, in effect, he "carried a cor-
rect mental photograph in his mind . . . for practically 18 months, when
he only had a glance in which to take this photograph."

The Pelser Motion

Another motion involved the testimony of prosecution witness
Lewis Pelser. In February 1922 Pelser—who had testified that he had
seen the shooting, and that a man he described as "the dead image" of
Sacco had shot Berardelli—met with Moore and gave him an affidavit
retracting his testimony. He had not been looking out the factory window, but had ducked beneath a workbench when the shooting started.
This is what Pelser had told the defense before the trial; at the trial he
had said he was looking out the window, and under cross-examination
explained the lie as a way to avoid being called as a witness. Now in his
affidavit Pelser said the prosecution had pressured him to identify Sacco
as the gunman.

Pelser had already changed his testimony enough to discredit it. But
the day after he gave Moore this affidavit retracting his story, he wrote
to Katzmann, telling him he had changed his testimony. But Pelser told
Katzmann that Moore had taken him to dinner and given him money,
and that he had been drinking heavily before writing the new affidavit.
Pelser retracted his retraction. Judge Thayer said that Pelser's frequent
changes in his story made him totally unreliable as a witness, and Thayer
would not call for a new trial based on the affidavit of such a person.

The Goodridge Motion

Yet another motion for a new trial addressed the testimony of Witness Carlos Goodridge. Goodridge had testified that he was coming out of a poolroom when he heard shots, and that Sacco had shot at him from the getaway car. Moore had asked Goodridge in court if he was then a defendant in that very court in another pending case. Goodridge answered no, and the prosecution objected to the question. However, Moore learned after the trial that Goodridge had a long criminal record involving passing bad checks and other offenses, and that his real name was Erastus Whitney. Shortly before the Sacco and Vanzetti trial Katzmann had prosecuted Whitney, or Goodridge, for grand larceny. Goodridge had entered a plea bargain, and at the time he testified at Sacco and Vanzetti's trial he was on probation. Moore argued that Goodridge's criminal record showed he was not a trustworthy witness, and that the fact he was on probation meant that he was potentially subject to pressure from the prosecution in order to avoid a prison sentence. Judge Thayer dismissed these objections to Goodridge's testimony; his convictions for passing bad checks were more than ten years old, and so could not be used (under Massachusetts law) to impeach his veracity. Thayer also would not allow the implication that Katzmann might improperly influence a witness.

The Andrews Motion

The defense also moved for a new trial based on the testimony of Lola Andrews. Judge Thayer acknowledged that allegations Moore raised about Andrews's testimony troubled him. Before the trial Andrews had told Moore that Sacco was not the man she had asked for directions outside the Slater & Morrill office. At the trial, she denied making this statement. Moore learned after the trial that Mrs. Andrews had a long record of insurance fraud and prostitution, and she was afraid that her past would be disclosed to her teenage son who was then living in Maine. A neighbor told Moore that the prosecutor had pressured Lola Andrews to identify Sacco as the man she had asked for directions. Moore got her to sign an affidavit retracting her testimony.

Judge Thayer said what bothered him about the Andrews affidavit was that it suggested unprofessional conduct by lawyers for both the prosecution and the defense. He said that he gave no credibility to the part of the affidavit in which Mrs. Andrews said that the prosecution had pressured her to identify Sacco. He viewed Moore's actions, though, as improperly coercive. An affidavit procured by intimidation and duress was not to be believed, he said, in dismissing this motion for a new trial.

The Hamilton Motion

The sixth motion related to the ballistics evidence. Self-professed ballistics expert Albert Hamilton contacted Moore in February 1923 and offered to examine the fatal bullet. He said that he had access to a new, more powerful microscope than had been used by the experts at the trial. Moore asked Hamilton to determine whether the fatal bullet and the "Fraher shell" had come from Sacco's gun. Hamilton measured the scratches on Bullet III and on the test bullets. His conclusion, based on the marks on the bullet, was that it could not have come from Sacco's gun. Also, said Hamilton, Sacco's gun had an imperfection on the firing pin, which left a mark on each of the three test shells. There was no such mark on the Fraher shell. This convinced Hamilton that neither Bullet III nor the Fraher shell had been fired by Sacco's gun.

The prosecution responded with an affidavit from Charles Van Amburgh, the Remington Company engineer who had testified at the trial. Van Amburgh's measurements differed slightly from Hamilton's— within the range to be expected given different atmospheric conditions on the measurement day—and he concluded that Bullet III was fired by Sacco's gun. He could reach no conclusion about the Fraher shell.

Moore also presented an affidavit from William Proctor, the prosecution's main ballistics witness. Proctor had written this affidavit in October 1923, saying that he had repeatedly told Katzmann before the trial that he did not believe Sacco's gun had fired Bullet III. He said he told Katzmann that if he were asked if he had any evidence that the fatal bullet came from Sacco's pistol, he would answer in the negative. He said that during the trial Katzmann had carefully phrased his questions to elicit a less unfavorable answer. In his affidavit, Proctor explained that this was why he had testified only that the marks on Bullet III showed that it "was consistent with" having been fired by a Colt pistol. He was unable, at the trial, to volunteer his opinion that the bullet did not come from this particular Colt pistol.

Katzmann submitted an affidavit denying that Proctor had expressed any pretrial doubts about Bullet III. Also, the trial transcript showed that the question Proctor answered was "Have you formed an opinion . . . whether . . . Bullet III was fired from that particular Colt automatic?" The question, Katzmann said, was not about Colt pistols in general. This discrepancy in the testimony was not addressed at the hearing, and Proctor died in March 1924, before Judge Thayer ruled on the motion. However, Judge Thayer dismissed the motion—he said to grant it on the basis of the Proctor affidavit would be equivalent to accusing the district attorney of perjury. Judge Thayer said he could not accuse Katzmann of perjury based on an affidavit from a dead man.

JUDGE THAYER DENIED ALL OF THESE defense motions on October 1, 1924, and the defendants appealed three of his decisions to the Massachusetts Supreme Judicial Court, which ultimately rejected them all in May 1926.

While these appeals were pending—in November 1925—the defense obtained an even more compelling piece of evidence. Celestino Medeiros was in the Dedham jail awaiting an appeal for his 1924 conviction for the murder of a bank guard. He passed a note to his fellow inmate Nicola Sacco that read: "I hear by confess to being in the south Braintree shoe company crime and Sacco and Vanzetti were not in said crime." Lawyer William G. Thompson interviewed Medeiros, who stated in an affidavit that he was part of the Morelli gang, who were "some Italians" who were wanted for thefts from several freight trains in early 1920—including one near the Slater & Morrill factory. He said that he had been one of the gunmen who stayed in the getaway car. He refused to identify the others in the gang, other than by first names.

After he gave this deposition, Medeiros was interviewed several times, by both the prosecution and the defense, and told an interesting story. He said that on the morning of April 15, 1920, he had been picked up at his home in Providence, Rhode Island, by four Italians—he did not know or would not disclose their names—in a Hudson. They drove to Boston, where they got some information about the holdup they were planning, and then they drove to Randolph, where they changed to the Buick. Although he claimed to have been at the scene and participated in the crime, he was unable to give any concrete details about the actual event—where the car waited, where the gunmen stood or approached the victims, what the crime scene looked like, or any landmarks along the escape route. He thought the payroll was in one black bag, and did not recall seeing any boxes. The defense team followed up on the Medeiros information and interviewed Joe Morelli and three of his brothers. Each of them denied knowing Medeiros and any involvement in the Braintree shootings. Medeiros received a new trial for the bank robbery murder, was convicted a second time, and was eventually executed—the same night as Sacco and Vanzetti.

ALMOST FROM THE TIME OF THEIR ARREST, there had been two parallel efforts to defend Sacco and Vanzetti. One was the legal effort—the team of lawyers who represented the defendants at the trial, filed numerous motions for a new trial, and appealed the convictions and the denials of their motions to the highest courts in the land. The other effort was directed at rallying public opinion.

Carlo Tresca, a colleague from the anarchist movement, started the Sacco and Vanzetti Defense Committee within days of their arrest in 1920. The public relations effort expanded rapidly, however, once Fred Moore was hired. The original purpose of the Defense Committee's public relations effort was to raise money for the legal expenses. After the trial, however, the committee began a propaganda campaign, designed to convince the courts to grant a new trial or the governor of Massachusetts to grant clemency, to commute their sentences, or even to pardon Sacco and Vanzetti. During the five years after the trial the committee distributed tens of thousands of pamphlets and broadsides describing the trial and the appeals efforts. Titles included "The Story of the Sacco-Vanzetti Case" (1921); "Victory Is in Sight," "The Fight Continues," Vanzetti's autobiographical "The Story of a Proletarian Life" (1924); and "Sacco and Vanzetti Speak to Judge Thayer: The Fearless Words of Two Innocent Men, Victims of a Legalized 'Frame-up': A Dramatic Picture of America Perverted" (1927).

Part of Moore's strategy was to make Sacco and Vanzetti martyrs to the cause of labor, and labor unions came to their support. The *Locomotive Engineers Journal* described Sacco and Vanzetti as "two Italian workingmen—labor organizers" wrongly convicted, and the Amalgamated Food Workers and Amalgamated Clothing Workers urged solidarity among all workers in fighting to overturn the convictions. The American Federation of Labor passed resolutions at its national conventions, arguing that Sacco and Vanzetti were innocent victims of prejudice.

Moore's strategy played on the radical political fervor of the early 1920s, and the Sacco-Vanzetti case soon became an international cause. Labor organizations and radical groups around the world demonstrated to protest the verdicts. Marches turned to violence in 1921 and 1922 in Paris, Brussels, Zurich, and Rome. In 1925 the American branch of the Communist Party adopted the Sacco and Vanzetti case as one of its main issues. Some observers suggested that guilt or innocence was not important to the Communists— the case was an opportunity for the party to show its support for the oppressed workingmen and provided a platform on which to build broad public recognition of its work.

Civil liberties groups—the New England Civil Liberties Committee and the newly formed American Civil Liberties Union— worked to keep public attention on the case. Various literary figures wrote letters to Judge Thayer, to the governor of Massachusetts (Channing H. Cox through 1926, Alvan T. Fuller in 1927), and to the editors of many newspapers. Analytical articles and editorials appeared in such magazines as *Outlook*, *The New Republic*, *Literary Digest*, and *The Nation*. Upton Sinclair's novel *Boston*, published in 1928, blasted the trial; and Henry Harrison published an anthology of poetry written about the case in 1927.

Though the Defense Committee made a powerful case for a new trial, the Supreme Judicial Court in 1926 refused to grant one. Their denial, however, renewed public interest in the Sacco and Vanzetti case.

The intensity of all of the public relations, public protest, and letter-writing efforts increased rapidly after the court's decision was announced. The Sacco and Vanzetti Defense Committee began to publish a monthly "Official Bulletin" with articles about the case. Labor unions, civil liberties groups, and bar associations passed further resolutions or filed protests—the arguments were about miscarriages of justice, oppression of the working class, discrimination against foreigners, and capital punishment. Anarchist groups called for general strikes or popular uprisings, but with no results.

Harvard law professor Felix Frankfurter (later a justice on the U.S. Supreme Court) carefully reviewed all the evidence in a March 1927 article in the *Atlantic Monthly*. Frankfurter argued in this article—which was later expanded into a book—that Sacco and Vanzetti were entitled to a new trial before a new judge. He contrasted the testimony of the primary eyewitnesses who had identified Sacco and Vanzetti with conflicting statements these same witnesses had made either before or after the trial. He also showed how Judge Thayer had presented Captain Proctor's equivocal testimony about Bullet III as gospel. Frankfurter also addressed at length the antiforeigner, antiradical prejudice that Judge Thayer had allowed the prosecutor to inflame.

Despite all of this public outcry, or perhaps to show that justice could not be swayed by popular sentiment, the Massachusetts Supreme Judicial Court on April 5, 1927, affirmed Judge Thayer's rejection of the defense's various appeals for a new trial—including the appeal for a new trial based on Medeiros's confession. Under Massachusetts law at the time, a trial judge did not pass sentence on the defendants until all appeals were completed. Now that the Supreme Judicial Court had affirmed Thayer's rulings, on April 9, 1927, Thayer sentenced Sacco and Vanzetti to die in the electric chair during the week beginning July 10, 1927.

CHAPTER FIVE

Sentencing and Execution

efore Judge Thayer passed sentence on April 9, 1927, he asked each defendant if he had "anything to say why sentence of death should not be passed."

"Yes, sir," Nicola Sacco began. "I am not an orator. It is not very familiar with me the English language," but "[my] comrade Vanzetti will speak more long, so I thought to give him the chance." Sacco would say relatively little—he "would like to tell all my life, but what is the use? You know all about what I say," and "you still today sentence us to death." Sacco thanked all the people who had been with him and Vanzetti for their seven-year ordeal, and concluded: "Judge Thayer know all my life, and he know that I am never been guilty, never—not yesterday nor today nor forever."

Then it was Bartolomeo Vanzetti's turn, and he would speak for nearly an hour. "Yes," he began when Sacco had concluded. "What I say is that I am innocent, not only of the Braintree crime, but also of the Bridgewater crime. That I am not only innocent of these two crimes, but in my life I have never stole and I have never killed and I have never spilled blood. That is what I want to say. And it is not all. Not only am I innocent of these two crimes, not only in all my life I have never stole, never killed, never spilled blood, but I have struggled all my life since I began to reason, to eliminate crime from the earth."

This, Vanzetti knew, was the reason he was now being put to death. He had struggled not only against the crimes "the official law and the official moral condemns, but also the crime that the official law and the official moral sanctions and sanctifies—the exploitation and oppression of the man by the man, and if there is a reason why I am here as a guilty man, if there is a reason why you in a few minutes can doom me, it is this reason and none else."

Vanzetti glanced at a paper, and continued. He spoke for a few minutes about Eugene Debs, the Socialist leader who had died the previous year. One of the last acts in Debs's life was to send a donation to the Sacco and Vanzetti Defense Committee, and he had said a chicken-killing dog would not have been convicted with the evidence Massachusetts had used against the men. Debs understood the course of American justice—for his opposition to the Great War he had been sent to the Atlanta penitentiary. "Just because he wanted the world a little better," Vanzetti said, "he was persecuted and slandered from his boyhood to his old age." But Debs, "the more good man I ever cast my eyes upon since I lived" will "last and will grow always more near and more dear to the people," Vanzetti predicted, "so long as admiration for goodness and for sacrifice will last."

Having praised the best man he had ever seen, Vanzetti turned to one of the worst. "I am sorry to say this," he said to Judge Thayer, "because you are an old man, and I have an old father," but "there could not have been another judge on the face of the earth more prejudiced and more cruel than you have been against us." Vanzetti and Sacco knew after seven years that Thayer had "been against us from the very beginning, before you see us." He had spoken against them with his friends "on the train, at the University Club of Boston, on the Golf Club of Worcester." Judge Thayer showed his prejudice, Vanzetti continued, when he told the jury in the Plymouth trial that "my crimes were in accordance with my principles." For this reason, Vanzetti said, the judge had sentenced him to twelve to fifteen years in prison for an attempted robbery, a longer sentence than any of the robbers in Charlestown prison had received.

Vanzetti did not blame the judge entirely—had he had more competent counsel at his first trial, had one of the McAnarney brothers, or William Thompson, defended him at that trial, "no jury would have found me guilty." But his first lawyer in Plymouth, John Vahey, was in alliance with Katzmann, and mounted a weak defense. The lawyer at their first trial in Dedham, Fred Moore, came from California and found Massachusetts afflicted with the notion that others "are not so good as they," and the other lawyers and jurors ostracized him. Vanzetti also acknowledged that the trials came at a moment of "hysteria of resentment and hate against the people of our principles, against the foreigner, against slackers," and Judge Thayer and Katzmann stirred the "passion of the juror, the prejudice of the juror, against us."

Vanzetti concluded by repeating that he was "not guilty of these two crimes," and that he had never stolen, killed, or spilled blood—and that he had fought against crime, both crimes condemned by law and the church, and crimes sanctified by law and the church. "This is what I say: I would not wish to a dog or to a snake" to suffer the way he and Sacco had, for crimes they had not committed. He was not guilty of the crimes for which he was about to be sentenced.

But in seven years Vanzetti had had much time to think about the workings of the justice system. And now his conclusion was somewhat different. "But my conviction is that I have suffered for things that I am guilty of. I am suffering because I am a radical and indeed I am a radical; I have suffered because I was an Italian, and indeed I am an Italian; I have suffered more for my family and my beloved [Sacco] than for myself; but I am so convinced to be right that if you could execute me two times, and if I could be reborn two other times, I would live again to do what I have done already."

Judge Thayer then began to pass sentence: Sacco would be electrocuted during the week of July 10. Vanzetti tried to interrupt, as he had more to say—the judge cut him off—and Sacco shouted, "You know I am innocent. That is the same words I pronounced seven years ago. You condemn two innocent men." The judge continued, also sentencing Vanzetti to die in the electric chair during the week of July 10, and adjourned the court.

The next day Vanzetti gave to friends the notes of what he had wanted to add to his statement—in his lengthy speech, he had talked "a great deal of myself but I even forgot to name Sacco." Sacco was "a heart, a faith, a character, a man; a man lover of nature and of mankind. A man who gave all, who sacrifice all to the cause of Liberty and to his love for mankind," sacrificing himself, his lovely wife and two beautiful children. Vanzetti acknowledged being "more witful" and a "better babbler than he is," but in contemplating Sacco's sacrifice of family "I feel small at the presence of his greatness. . . ." He warned Judge Thayer that "Sacco's name will live in the hearts of the people and in their gratitude when Katzmann's and your bones will be dispersed by time, when your name, his name, your laws, institutions, and your false god are but *a deem rememoring of a cursed past in which man was wolf to the man.* . . ."

"If it had not been for this thing," Vanzetti told a reporter, "I might have live out my life, talking at street corners to scorning men. I might have die, unmarked, unknown, a failure. Now we are not a failure. This is our career and our triumph. Never in our full life can we hope to do such work for tolerance, for justice, for man's understanding of man, as now we do by an accident. Our words—our lives—our pains—nothing! The taking of our lives—lives of a good shoemaker and a poor fish-peddler—all! The last moment belongs to us—the agony is our triumph!"

Vanzetti knew that his life—that of a poor fish-peddler spending his idle moments talking on street corners to scorning men—would have amounted to little. As an orator and writer for *Cronaca Sovversiva* he had not stirred the masses to revolt against the oppressive state. But as a victim of a judicial murder, he had become much more than another street-corner orator. More, his ability to express himself in these few words, which one novelist called the noblest "heard in America in the two generations since Abraham Lincoln died," stirred hearts as could no revolutionary pamphlet.

The anarchists had been the first to come to Sacco and Vanzetti's defense. But now radicals of all kinds—Socialists, Communists, labor organizers—joined the cause. Intellectuals joined in—Professor John Dewey, pioneer of American education, wrote in support of Sacco and Vanzetti; novelist John Dos Passos volunteered at the Sacco and Vanzetti Defense Committee; poets Edna St. Vincent Millay and Dorothy Parker were arrested at demonstrations in front of the Massachusetts state house. In addition to the radicals and intellectuals, Sacco and Vanzetti found their strongest supporters among some conservative members of the American bar. Boston lawyer William G. Thompson became their attorney after their conviction in July 1921; he remained their lawyer until August 1927.

The Sacco and Vanzetti Defense Committee brought together this diverse coalition—some leftists, some Boston Brahmins—to either save Sacco and Vanzetti or to ensure that their voices would be heard. It was never clear which was the ultimate goal—to save their lives, or to use their deaths to attack the American system of justice. Among the committee members differences sometimes flared, and the various elements of the coalition—Communists, Socialists, anarchists—would hold separate rallies on Boston Common. The Communists gathered under one tree to rally for Sacco and Vanzetti, the Socialists another, and the anarchists a third.

From its headquarters on Hanover Street in Boston's North End, the committee also published scores of pamphlets on various aspects of the case as well as Bartolomeo Vanzetti's autobiography, *Story of a Proletarian Life.* Though the Boston papers for the most part shunned

Mary Donovan of the Sacco and Vanzetti Defense Committee protesting the death sentence on Boston Common, August 1927 (courtesy of the Massachusetts Archives)

the radicals, with so many high-powered writers interested in the case, the story of Sacco and Vanzetti was told and retold around the world. Boston's papers almost universally took the position that the two were guilty, and that justice had been done. Defenders of Sacco and Vanzetti held that the two were framed for their political views. Yes, the two men were radicals, and they had been involved with groups that were implicated in dynamite plots in 1919 and 1920—but they were not only innocent of any violent deeds but had never had any violent thoughts. Though Upton Sinclair presented the case clearly and Vanzetti sympathetically in his 1928 novel *Boston*, some radicals criticized him for suggesting that the anarchists had in fact been part of the violent Galleanist movement.

But it became clear to anyone who looked at the record candidly that whatever involvement Sacco and Vanzetti may have had in the dynamite attacks, they were not involved in either the Bridgewater or the Braintree robberies. William Thompson, their lawyer, petitioned Governor Alvan T. Fuller for clemency. Though the petition was on behalf of both Vanzetti and Sacco, the latter refused to sign. He had reconciled himself to the idea that the state would kill him no matter what; he also thought that Rosina had been through enough trauma and stress—if his life were resolved and over, she would be able to move on with hers.

Governor Fuller, a Republican and owner of one of New England's largest car dealerships (the family business he began is still carried on by his son Peter Fuller), conducted his own investigation into the case. He summoned witnesses, with no counsel present except the governor's personal lawyer. A package bomb sent to Fuller on May 10 did not make Fuller any more sympathetic to the anarchists, but Thompson and more conservative members of the Defense Committee objected to this "star chamber" proceeding. Under great public pressure, Governor Fuller on June 1 announced that he had appointed a three-man commission to review the case. President A. Lawrence Lowell of Harvard, President Samuel Stratton of M.I.T., and novelist and retired Judge Robert Grant, formerly of the state probate court, would review the case record. Thompson objected immediately—neither Lowell nor Stratton was a lawyer, and Grant had already expressed his hostility both to Italians generally, in his books, and to Sacco and Vanzetti, privately, to anyone who would listen. But the eminence of Stratton and Lowell, and their apparent impartiality, was sufficient for most observers without a direct stake in the case.

Governor Fuller continued his own investigation while the Lowell Committee began its work, though Lowell and Stratton could not arrange to meet until after Harvard and M.I.T. had their June commencements. The committee, like the governor, saw no need to include the lawyers for Sacco and Vanzetti, nor did it see a need to hold public hearings. Lowell, Stratton, and Grant began their proceedings, holding hearings for ten days between July 11 and July 21, 1927, recalling witnesses—including Judge Thayer and the eleven surviving jurors. Governor Fuller postponed the date of execution to August 10, giving both the committee and himself time to review all the evidence.

The Lowell Committee focused on a number of key points: the prejudice of Judge Thayer, the weight of the evidence, and the extent to which the defendants' radical views influenced the verdict against them. On this last point, the committee ultimately ruled that since the defense had introduced these political views at the trial, the defense should not complain that the jury took these views into account. On the first point, the committee criticized Judge Thayer (whom they had questioned privately, without the defense lawyers present) for expressing his opinions about the defendants outside of court. But the committee did not think Thayer's private opinions influenced the trial.

On the weight of the evidence the committee also found that Sacco and Vanzetti were not tried unfairly. The committee recalled many of the witnesses, including some who had not testified at the 1921 trial. One, Carlotta Packard Tattillo, testified that she had known Sacco in 1908, when she and he both worked at the Rice & Hutchins shoe factory, and he had thrown a shoe last at her. She said she spoke to him on the street on April 15, 1920. As Lottie Tattillo grew hysterical, accusing Thompson of trying to attack her character, District Attorney Dudley Ranney explained that the prosecution had not called her at the trial because she was so unstable and unreliable. Specifically, the prosecution could find no evidence that Sacco worked at Rice & Hutchins in 1908—a key part of her story. Braintree police chief Jeremiah Gallivan told the committee that he knew Lottie Tattillo, and she was "a nut." Why she was called no one knew, and though she might

Lawrence Lowell, president of Harvard University and head of a commission that reviewed Sacco and Vanzetti's case (courtesy of the Massachusetts Archives)

have provided comic relief, her testimony to the Lowell Committee—about the shoe throwing, which seemed to indicate Sacco had a violent side—helped send Sacco and Vanzetti to the electric chair.

Chief Gallivan, who had retired the previous year after twenty-one years running the Braintree Police Department, also testified about the cap that had been identified as Sacco's at the first trial. Katzmann had shown it was Sacco's by the hole in the lining—a hole, he argued, made by Sacco's habit of hanging it on the same nail every day at the Three-K factory. At the Lowell Committee hearing, Gallivan examined the hat and remembered the hole—in fact, he told the committee that he had torn the hole in the lining to see if he could find any identification. Katzmann had used this same hole to show that the hat was on Sacco's head.

Felice Guadagni, a journalist and literary scholar, had testified that he and Albert Bosco, editor of *La Notizia*, had eaten lunch with Sacco at Boni's restaurant in the North End on April 15, 1920. He left Sacco at about 1:30 and saw him later, at about 3:00, at Giordano's coffeehouse. He was sure of the date because they discussed a banquet the Italian journalists were holding to honor the editor of the *Boston Transcript*. This would have been a memorable occasion—Italian reporters breaking bread with "a gentleman from the *Transcript*." Guadagni remembered that the great event was to happen on April 15, and that he had invited Sacco to come along.

Stratton, though, had called John Williams, now in Washington, who remembered that the banquet was in May. Though Williams did not testify, the committee had his word that the banquet had not happened on April 15. Lowell announced that a serious Sacco alibi had been destroyed.

"I was so sure of that day," Guadagni said. The committee knew that Guadagni was treasurer of the Sacco and Vanzetti Defense Committee, and hanging over the room was their suspicion that he would lie to save a fellow radical. Why, Lowell wanted to know, had Guadagni testified about the banquet on April 15 when it had not happened on that date? Why had he lied at the trial and before the committee? Guadagni distinctly remembered talking about the banquet on the fifteenth, but the more he talked about it to the committee, the more they were sure he was lying.

Guadagni left the committee hearing feeling destroyed. Lowell said that Sacco's alibi had also been destroyed. At the committee's suggestion, Bosco looked into the files of *La Notizia*. There, in the issue dated April 16, 1920, they found an article about the dinner given for Williams at a North End priory on April 15, 1920.

Lowell announced "that a mistake had been made." It turned out that Williams was mistaken; Guadagni and Bosco had been remembering correctly. Lowell apologized to Guadagni and Bosco, but their truthfulness did not make him believe that Sacco had been in Boston, rather than in Braintree, on April 15, 1920.

The defense scoured other sources for more evidence, more witnesses. Herbert Ehrmann, assisting Thompson with the defense, talked with every fish dealer at the Fish Pier in South Boston and along

Atlantic Avenue to find the one who had sold eels to Vanzetti. They finally found him—but his records only went back a year or so. They asked if they could look. Up to the loft they went, opening box after box of receipts, ledger books, and scrap papers. In the last box, the last receipt was dated January 1920. Was there anything earlier? Shoved into the rafters in the cramped and sweltering storeroom they found another box—with receipts from 1919. Finally, December, and a slip for a barrel of eels shipped on December 20, 1919, to B. Vanzetti of Plymouth. The eels were to arrive in Plymouth on December 23 for delivery the next day. All of the alibi evidence for Vanzetti had been verbal—the Italians of Plymouth who remembered him selling them eels on Christmas Eve. Now here was a paper trail. Ehrmann took the paper, made a photostatic copy, and raced to the governor's office. The governor's secretary simply asked if Ehrmann had any evidence that Vanzetti had received the eels.

The committee and the governor also discounted the testimony of Celestino Medeiros, who had confessed to being involved with the Braintree crime. Judge Thayer had rejected the story Medeiros told, finding him to be "without doubt, a crook, a thief, a robber, a liar, a rum-runner, a 'bouncer' in a house of ill-fame, a smuggler," and already sentenced to death for killing a bank cashier. However, Thayer said, Medeiros did not recall any of the details about the Braintree robbery scene, which suggested that he was making up his confession for some unknown reason. Both the governor and the committee made much of the fact that there was not enough evidence to convict Medeiros of murdering either Parmenter or Berardelli; therefore, there would be no reason to charge him with complicity and find the men he said were responsible for the deaths.

Governor Fuller called in John J. Richards, the adjutant general of Rhode Island, who as a U.S. Marshal in 1920 had investigated the Morelli gang. Richards began telling the governor about the Morelli gang, whose descriptions and modus operandi matched those of the Braintree robbers. The governor cut him off—he was not interested in these Rhode Island thugs. What did Richards know about the Braintree murders? Richards knew nothing of the Braintree case, so Fuller dismissed him. Richards told Thompson and Ehrmann that their clients were as good as dead; Governor Fuller did not care about the Medeiros evidence.

Medeiros recalled that the governor began the fifteen-minute interview by saying he knew Medeiros thought he had been given "a raw deal," but perhaps if he cooperated the governor could do something for him. Immediately after saying this the governor had asked, "You don't know anything about the Sacco-Vanzetti case, do you?" Medeiros said he did, and said he had been in the car at the Braintree robbery and murder. "So you are a double murderer," Governor Fuller said. "I will do nothing for you."

The Lowell Committee issued its report on July 27, 1927. It criticized Thayer mildly for expressing himself out of court, but "on the whole" it found that Sacco and Vanzetti had received a fair trial, and the evidence the committee had reviewed sustained the jury's verdict. Governor Fuller announced that he would render his own decision — whether to grant clemency or call for a new trial—on August 3.

Fuller found no reason to call for a new trial. His statement, on August 3, was intended to reassure the "sober-minded and conscientious men and women who were genuinely troubled about the guilt or innocence of the accused and the fairness of the trial." He explained why he had appointed the Lowell Committee as well as why he had conducted his own investigation—"to see from a layman's standpoint" whether the trial was fair. Now, Fuller was convinced that it was. He had spoken with the jurors, and if Thayer was biased, "he gave them no indication of his own opinion of the case."

As for Medeiros, Fuller discounted his confession. "It is popularly supposed he confessed to committing this crime. In his testimony to me he could not recall the details or describe the neighborhood." Actually, Medeiros had confessed not to the murder itself, but to being in the car that pulled off the Braintree crime—he had been in the curtained-in back seat. Moreover, in his various statements, Medeiros could recall whether the car was traveling up hill or down at different points of the route, and his recollection of its travels squared with the route taken from Braintree to Bridgewater. Fuller, however, continued: "He furthermore stated that the government had doublecrossed him and he proposes to doublecross the government." Fuller reasoned that Medeiros, upset that he was sentenced to death for killing a Wrentham bank teller while his two confederates in the robbery were given life in prison, wanted to spare the anarchists because doing so would embarrass the Commonwealth, which had invested so much in their trial and conviction.

None of the defense's evidence was working. Fuller saw no reason to give Sacco and Vanzetti a new trial, and he set their execution for August 10. Thompson stepped down as their counsel, thinking that a new lawyer, one who had not made so many enemies in defending them, might be able to spare them. The Defense Committee engaged Arthur D. Hill, one of Boston's most eminent attorneys, to handle the case. Hill filed motions to revoke the sentence. Hill argued that Judge Thayer was prejudiced, and therefore a new trial should be granted. On August 6, Hill petitioned to have a judge other than Thayer hear the motion, but Chief Judge Walter Perley Hall of the Massachusetts Supreme Judicial Court denied this petition, ruling that motions for a new trial were always heard by the judge who had presided at the first trial. On August 8, Hill argued before Judge Thayer that he should grant a new trial for Sacco and Vanzetti because he, Thayer, had been prejudiced from the outset. Thayer denied the motion.

A wave of bombings on August 6—in the New York subway, a church in Philadelphia, and the mayor of Baltimore's home—strengthened Thayer's resolve to stamp out the radical threat. The Sacco and Vanzetti Defense Committee charged that these bombings were the work of the police saboteurs, trying to discredit their campaign.

Hill turned again to the Supreme Judicial Court for a writ of error, and was denied. He also appealed to the Supreme Court of the United States, seeking a writ of habeas corpus from Oliver Wendell Holmes, Jr., of the U.S. Supreme Court. Holmes thought he had no authority to issue a writ—"prejudice on the part of the presiding judge however strong" would not deprive the court of its "legal power to decide the case," and so denied the writ. Federal district judge George Anderson agreed.

At 8 P.M. on August 10, Hill was at the State House, arguing for more time with the governor, asking the Governor's Council to grant clemency. As Sacco and Vanzetti were led to the death chamber just before midnight, Governor Fuller granted them twelve more days to argue their case to the Supreme Judicial Court of Massachusetts. The day before Hill argued his case, a bomb destroyed the East Milton home of one of the original jurors, throwing the juror, his wife, and three children from their beds but not seriously injuring them. The Supreme Judicial Court heard the arguments on August 16, and three days later denied Hill's request.

Arthur Hill drove to Beverly Farms to ask Justice Oliver Wendell Holmes for a writ of certiorari, so the Supreme Court could review the entire record of the case. Holmes was sympathetic: "I am far from saying that I think counsel was not warranted in presenting the question raised," but Holmes did not think "there was a reasonable chance" the entire Supreme Court would "ultimately reverse the judgment." He had "received many letters from people who seem to suppose that I have a general discretion to see that justice is done."

Holmes said he did not have this discretion, and denied the application. Hill got back into his car and drove to Chatham, on Cape Cod, to see Justice Louis D. Brandeis. Brandeis was the great hope of all defenders of Sacco and Vanzetti. But he, too, would have to deny the application—because Rosina Sacco had rented a Dedham house from his wife, and because his wife and daughter had shown a great interest in the case, Brandeis felt he might be prejudiced in favor of the defense and so could not intervene.

Hill would not give up; he took a boat to the vacation home of Justice Harlan Stone, on an island off the Maine coast. Stone concurred "in the view expressed by Justice Holmes as to the merits of the application," but denied granting a stay. Chief Justice William Howard Taft, vacationing in Canada, refused a request to return to American soil to consider the application.

At Sacco and Vanzetti Defense Committee headquarters on Hanover Street, Felix Frankfurter told an organizer, out of Rosina Sacco's hearing, that "[s]he must not be made conscious of the larger issues of this thing, for now how can she think of anything but that it is her loved one who suffers! Yet somehow, no matter what happens tonight, I am too healthy—or something—to give up hope. I cannot believe it is the end."

Hill could not give up, nor could Frankfurter. As the lawyers tried to save the condemned men, as the Defense Committee rallied in the North End, Luigia Vanzetti arrived from Italy. She came in time to see her brother, the first time in nineteen years, for one last visit in the Charlestown prison.

At midnight, guards woke Celestino Medeiros, who had been

Series of cartoons that appeared in the **Daily Worker** *in July and August 1927, in the days before Sacco and Vanzetti's execution (courtesy of the Michigan State University Libraries)*

sleeping away the final hours of his life. The guards led him to the chair. Medeiros was strapped into the chair and blindfolded, the warden raised his hand, and executioner Robert G. Elliott of New York—who was paid his travel expenses and $250 for each death—moved the switch. At nine minutes, thirty-five seconds after midnight, now August 23, Medeiros was dead.

Then Sacco was taken from his cell. He walked directly to the chair, not needing an escort, and as the attendants strapped him in he rose slightly to say, "Viva l'anarchia!" When the straps and blindfold were firmly in place he spoke again: "Farewell, my wife and children and all my friends!" And as the warden prepared to signal the executioner: "Good evening, gentlemen. Farewell, Mother."

Twenty-one hundred volts jolted through Nicola Sacco's body. Nineteen minutes and two seconds after midnight he was pronounced dead.

Now the guards came for Vanzetti. He was sitting on his cot, where he had spent much of the evening reading Charles and Mary Beard's *Rise of American Civilization*. Each guard took one arm to walk him to the death chamber. When they entered the chamber they released him, and Vanzetti turned to each man. "Goodbye," he said, shaking each man by the hand. He extended his hand to Warden William Hendry. "Warden, I want to thank you for all that you have done for me. I wish to tell you that I am innocent and that I have never committed any crime but sometimes sin. I thank you for everything you have done for me. I am innocent of all crime, not only of this, but all. I am an innocent man." They shook hands, then Vanzetti sat in the chair. After he had been securely strapped in and blindfolded, he spoke a final time: "I wish to forgive some people for what they are now doing to me."

The guards, the warden, even the executioner, were all men like him; caught in a bad system. The warden, raising the hand Vanzetti had just taken, signaled the executioner, and 1,950 volts shot through Bartolomeo Vanzetti's body. At twenty-six minutes, fifty-five seconds after midnight, August 23, 1927, he was dead.

Sacco and Vanzetti both died in the knowledge, the faith, that their deaths would help bring about a better world. But they also died believing their death would touch off an international revolution. News of the executions produced demonstrations and riots in Europe. A one-day general strike crippled Paris, and police and protestors fought brief gun battles. Mobs in Geneva overturned American cars and looted shops selling American goods. In Johannesburg, South Africa, protesters burned an American flag, and violence erupted in London, Mexico City, and Sydney. (An East German scholar researching in the Soviet Union archives in 1958 discovered that the Communist Party had instigated these "spontaneous demonstrations.")

Authorities in Boston tried to make sure this kind of violence would not erupt here. Efforts by the Defense Committee to get the bodies from the prison were resisted, and the prison officials planned to donate the corpses to Harvard Medical School. The lawyers fought this and had the bodies released to Rosina Sacco and Luigia Vanzetti, so the Defense Committee could organize its own funeral. But police and the landlord thwarted the committee's hope to have the bodies lie in state in their crowded offices at 256 Hanover Street by nailing a two-by-four upright in the middle of the doorway. Caskets could not be carried in.

Instead, the bodies were taken from Charlestown to Langone's Funeral Home in the North End. There, on the evening of August 25, eight thousand people crowded to view the bodies. Among the first mourners was Mary Donovan, for two years the recording secretary for the Sacco and Vanzetti Defense Committee. At the head of the caskets she held a copy of the placard she had been arrested for nailing up on the Common: "DID YOU SEE WHAT I DID TO THOSE ANARCHISTIC BASTARDS?—JUDGE THAYER."

Funeral director Joseph Langone, knowing his license would be suspended if there were trouble, ushered her outside, where she handed the sign to a newsman to copy. As he handed it back to her, a police officer seized it, and then arrested Mary for inciting a riot and distributing anarchist propaganda. The fact that Judge Thayer had written this particular piece of propaganda struck many as ironic.

Sunday, August 28, was rainy and cold as a November day. At one o'clock the Defense Committee planned its "March of Sorrow" to convey the bodies of Sacco and Vanzetti to Forest Hills Cemetery for cremation. Thousands gathered between Langone's and North End Park to begin the eight-mile procession. Rosina Sacco and her children rode in a car with Luigia Vanzetti; the Defense Committee rode in the second, following the hearses. The mounted police surrounding the hearses and cars

Two hearses carrying Sacco and Vanzetti from the funeral home to Forest Hills Cemetery as they passed Boston Common (courtesy of the Massachusetts Archives)

were not there as an honor guard. Behind came open cars carrying red flowers, followed by up to fifty thousand marchers. Police in the North End had forbidden the marchers to don their red armbands with the words: REMEMBER JUSTICE CRUCIFIED! AUGUST 22, 1927. Marchers put these in their pockets until they had crossed through Scollay Square.

In the blustery rain the mourners linked arms and marched down Hanover Street and into Scollay Square, where the police had parked heavy trucks to obstruct the parade, and here the police made their first charge into the line of marchers. An observer on the sidewalk was so shocked at the police attack he swore, and was immediately arrested. The marchers did not retaliate against the police, who hoped to provoke the marchers to fight back before witnesses, and thus allow indiscriminate clubbing and arrests. Instead the marchers, arms linked, continued to file through Scollay Square, where they put on their red armbands to follow the procession down Tremont to Boston Common.

A young man described as "100 percent American" stood at the corner of the Common watching the procession, amused at the obstacles the police found to put in the funeral's way. He smiled as the mounted police charged the marchers, then heard the growl of a police officer: "Hey you! Get away from there and run!" The young man began to walk away slowly. "Run, I told ye—and keep running! I'll smash your face in for you!" He ran, doubled back, and instead of watching decided to join the march. He told the mourners, "Now I know why you are fighting."

Unable to provoke a riot, the police found more subtle ways to disrupt the cortege—directing traffic into the walkers, sending streams of taxicabs—no one knew where such a procession of cabs was heading on a rainy Sunday afternoon—through the procession, parking trucks in the path. Near the Forest Hills elevated train station the police made another charge, this time with a car driving into the crowd. This sent all but a few hundred hearty survivors fleeing, until only a few hundred reached Forest Hills Cemetery.

Those who made it crowded into the chapel for a final goodbye to Sacco and Vanzetti before their bodies were cremated.

Mary Donovan rose to read a brief tribute, written by Gardner Jackson.

> Nicola Sacco and Bartolomeo Vanzetti, you came to America seeking freedom. In the strong idealism of youth you came as workers searching for that liberty and equality of opportunity heralded as the particular gift of this country to all new-comers. You centered your labors in Massachusetts, the very birthplace of American ideals. And now Massachusetts and America have killed you—murdered you because you were Italian anarchists.

Donovan spoke of the Salem witch trials of 1692. While the "shame of those old acts of barbarism can never be wiped out," she said they were "nothing beside this murder which modern Massachusetts has committed upon you." She said the witch-burners were blinded by the "superstitious fear of an emotional religion," but Sacco and Vanzetti's killers had acted "in deliberate cold blood." They had allowed class prejudice to blind them, and "cared more for wealth, comfort, and institutions than they did for truth." Sacco and Vanzetti were victims "of the crassest plutocracy the world has known since ancient Rome."

Donovan quoted what had become Vanzetti's testament, "If it had not been for these things, I might have lived out my life, talking at street corners to scorning men," and said that by Vanzetti's final "triumph we are fired with an everlasting fire. Your long years of torture and your last hours of supreme agony are the living banner under which we and our descendants for generations to come will march to accomplish that better world based on the brotherhood of man for which you died. In your martyrdom we will fight on and conquer."

Epilogue

Vanzetti had seen their deaths as a triumph, thinking it would bring on a global revolution. Though Boston police did their best to prevent the revolution from breaking out at the funeral, the deaths of Sacco and Vanzetti inspired controversy around the world and for years to come.

In other parts of the world, the Communist Party used their execution for a renewed wave of violence and anti-American propaganda. Their deaths had been more useful than their lives would have been to the Communists in showing the barbarism of American justice.

The Sacco and Vanzetti Defense Committee had tenuously bonded anarchists, Socialists, Communists, Boston Brahmins, and intellectuals. Each group, each individual, had a different agenda. Sometimes they harmonized—all wanted a new trial, though some believed the state would be just as anxious to condemn Sacco and Vanzetti at a second trial as it had been at the first. Now that the two were dead, a new trial was out of the question, so the different factions drifted apart.

Anarchists attacked both the executioner and Judge Thayer in the years afterward. The home of Robert Elliott, the executioner, was damaged by a bomb in 1928, and on September 27, 1932, a bomb devastated Judge Thayer's house in Worcester. No one was ever charged in these bombings. Thayer moved to a men's club in Boston, where he died in 1933.

For the Italian anarchists, the real threat no longer was the American state, but the Italian government. Mussolini had come to power in 1922, ruthlessly crushing political opposition. The year Sacco and Vanzetti were executed, Mike Boda was arrested by the fascist regime in Italy and sentenced to five years imprisonment for radical activities. Young Dante Sacco, along with Edward Holton James from the Defense Committee, visited Boda in his Italian prison in 1932. After Boda's release that same year, he briefly acted as an informer, infiltrating radical groups in France and Switzerland. Other anarchists—notably Ferruccio Coacci—fled Italy for Argentina. Anarchists supported the Republicans in the Spanish Civil War, among the first to fight against the fascist insurgents. When the Soviet Union entered the Spanish Civil War on the same side, though, the Communists first executed many of the anarchists, eliminating their main rivals on the revolutionary left. Vanzetti and many other anarchists had regarded the Soviet regime to be as oppressive as the capitalist regimes they were fighting in the rest of the world. The Spanish Civil War proved them right.

Sacco and Vanzetti had become figures of international importance, but they were also individuals whose greatest impact was on their families, friends, and comrades. Rosina Sacco, with her son, Dante, and daughter, Inez, continued to live in the Boston area. During the campaign to free her husband she had worked tirelessly with the Defense Committee. Two years after her husband died, she and Ermanno Bianchini, one of the Defense Committee members, became companions, and they married in 1943, settling on a poultry farm in West Bridgewater. Still a committed anarchist, and bitter about the state that had executed her husband, Rosina refused to attend her daughter's wedding in a church, or her son's funeral. She survived into her nineties and continued to see the few surviving comrades, though she refused to talk about the case.

Mary Donovan could not find work after spending years on Sacco and Vanzetti's defense. In December 1927 she and Powers Hapgood, an associate from the Sacco and Vanzetti Defense Committee, married, and in 1928 Mary Donovan Hapgood was the Socialist candidate for governor of Massachusetts, the first woman to seek statewide office in the Commonwealth. She did not win, and she and her husband and children—they named their first child, a girl, Barta after Bartolomeo and Nicola—moved to a farm in Indiana, where both continued to write and organize.

Fifty poets, including Edna St.Vincent Millay, Countee Cullen, and John Dos Passos, contributed to *America Arraigned*, an anthology on the Sacco and Vanzetti case published by the Defense Committee.The title indicates the tenor of much of the literature published after their deaths.

Marion Denman Frankfurter and Gardner Jackson edited the *Letters of Sacco and Vanzetti*, which was published in 1928 and presented the two, in their own words, as imprisoned martyrs.

Sacco and Vanzetti have also been the subject of numerous dramatic productions, some performed on the Broadway stage. The earliest was in 1928; the most recent was in production as this book went to press.The earliest play, *Gods of the Lightning* by Maxwell Anderson, was a fictional portrayal of the trial. When the playwright sought to bring the play to Boston, he was told that the Licensing Division—we would call them "censors" today—would not allow it because it was "so condemnatory of our government" as to be "anarchistic and treasonable." Moreover, the play would "bring into disrepute our judicial officers . . . who participated in the Sacco-Vanzetti trial." In 1935 Anderson wrote another play, *Winterset*, which was also a fictionalized version of the case. This play had a successful run on Broadway and won the New York Drama Critics Award.

Woody Guthrie wrote and recorded a series of songs about the case in 1946 and 1947, which were collected and published on an album as *The Ballads of Sacco and Vanzetti*. The CD version of that album is still available today.

The Sacco-Vanzetti story inspired movies—both documentaries and dramatic productions. Armand Aulicino and Frank Field wrote a musical based on the case, *The Shoemaker and the Peddler*, which had a short run off Broadway in 1960 and again in 1969. In 1960 the Ford Foundation commissioned an opera based on the case. However, the author died before completing the work, and it has not yet been produced. Composer Marc Blitzstein began writing an opera, which was unfinished at the time of his death in 1964. Another composer later completed the work, which finally premiered in 2001.

Several productions played on both stage and television. NBC presented a two-hour television show based on the case in 1960. In 1963, Robert Nash's dramatic treatment of the trial and the appeals, *The Advocate*, was presented on television the same night it opened on Broadway.

Herbert Ehrmann published *The Untried Case* in 1933, in which he documented the Morelli gang's activities and argued that they were the real perpetrators. Massachusetts governor Joseph Ely read the book; when he began, Ely said, he had "some doubt" as to Sacco and Vanzetti's guilt; when he finished, "I had no doubt of their innocence." Since it was then six years after the executions, it was too late for Governor Ely to do anything in the case. However, the Commonwealth did move to make it more difficult for this kind of judicial miscarriage in the future. In 1939 Massachusetts changed the law so that criminal appeals would be heard by a judge other than the one who had conducted the case. The law also allowed the Supreme Judicial Court to grant a new trial if the jury verdict was against the weight of evidence or contradicted by newly discovered evidence. Under the old law, evidence turned up after a trial could not be used to clear the accused—the new law, passed in the wake of Sacco and Vanzetti's execution, would allow such evidence. Had Sacco and Vanzetti not been condemned and executed, despite the discovery of the Morelli gang, this law would not have been changed, and recent advances in DNA identification would not have been grounds to grant new trials for people wrongly convicted of crimes.

At the time of the executions, Justice Oliver Wendell Holmes had corrected the common misperception that he, as a member of the Supreme Court, had a general discretion to see that justice was done. In the 1920s, and before, the Supreme Court would rarely intervene in a state murder case. After the 1930s, the Supreme Court would more often review state court decisions, particularly if the accused had been denied one of the protections of the Bill of Rights. The Supreme Court also restricted what states could do to prohibit free speech, and in 1930 invalidated a Minnesota law punishing criminal anarchy.

On the tenth anniversary of the execution, sculptor Gutzon Borglum, who created the Mount Rushmore monument to Washington, Jefferson, Lincoln, and Theodore Roosevelt, created a small bas relief of Sacco and Vanzetti. It showed the two men in profile facing a lopsided set of scales, with "Law" outweighing "Justice," and carried a quotation from Vanzetti:

What I wish more than all in this last hour of agony is that our case and our fate may be understood in their real being and serve as a tremendous lesson to the forces of freedom so that our suffering and death shall not have been in vain.

Borglum hoped to present this as a monument to be placed in the Massachusetts State House, but Governor Charles Hurley refused to accept it. Mayor Fredrick Mansfield said the question was one for the City Council, but he would record his opposition. Ten years later, Borglum tried again to present his bas relief to be placed on Boston Common, and Governor Robert F. Bradford refused, saying he had no jurisdiction over Boston Common. Furthermore, said the governor, "I can see no useful purpose in stirring up the bitter passions and prejudices of twenty years ago." In 1957, both Governor Foster Furcolo and Boston mayor John F. Hynes rejected the offer.

The Massachusetts legislature considered a resolution to clear Sacco and Vanzetti's names in 1959—Mary Donovan Hapgood attended the legislative hearings wearing a death mask—but rejected the attempt.

Plaque sculpted by Gutzon Borglum, on the wall in the Boston Public Library (courtesy of the the Boston Public Library)

In 1977, as part of the fiftieth anniversary of the executions, Governor Michael Dukakis declared August 23, 1977, to be Sacco and Vanzetti Day. Dukakis had studied the idea of a pardon, but determined that a pardon of an executed person would suggest that Sacco and Vanzetti had actually committed the crimes for which they were executed. The governor now believed the two men were innocent. His proclamation called on the people of the Commonwealth to "reflect on these tragic events," and declared that "any stigma and disgrace should be forever removed from the names of Nicola Sacco and Bartolomeo Vanzetti," their families and descendants, and "from the name of the Commonwealth of Massachusetts." Governor Dukakis hoped that the people of Massachusetts would draw from the historic lesson of Sacco and Vanzetti "the resolve to prevent the forces of intolerance, fear, and hatred from ever again uniting to overcome the rationality, wisdom, and fairness to which our legal system aspires."

The Massachusetts Senate promptly voted to condemn the Governor's resolution.

The Boston Public Library has long had a collection of materials from the Sacco and Vanzetti case in its Rare Books Department. In 1979 Borglum's sculpture was quietly placed on a wall in a corridor on the library's third floor, just outside the Rare Books area, where it hangs today. In 1997, Acting Governor Paul Cellucci and Boston Mayor Thomas Menino—the two highest-ranking Massachusetts officials of Italian heritage—formally accepted the plaque. Mayor Menino suggested that the plaque—which is actually a plaster carving intended to be used for casting a work in bronze—be cast and installed in some more suitable location. The president of the Boston City Council, James Kelly, immediately announced he would oppose any expenditure of public funds for such a purpose.

A number of writers and historians have continued to examine the case and have written dozens of books and magazine articles. For nearly forty years after the executions, almost without exception, these authors have argued that Sacco and Vanzetti were innocent, and that they were victims of prejudice, of passion, or of a corrupt prosecution and judge. Upton Sinclair said that he decided to write *Boston: A Novel* (1928), a fictionalized version of the Sacco and Vanzetti case, the day before the executions. John Dos Passos, in his monumental trilogy, *U.S.A.* (1937), treats the case as a miscarriage of justice. Not until the late 1950s did there appear any serious literary efforts to support the prosecution.

The publication in 1960 of Robert Montgomery's *Sacco and Vanzetti: The Murder and the Myth* renewed the controversy, as Montgomery argued that Sacco and Vanzetti were in fact involved in the Braintree robbery and killings, and that the trial and the appellate process had been conducted fairly. This prompted Herbert Ehrmann to reissue his *The Untried Case*, with a brief new epilogue challenging Montgomery's arguments. Felix Frankfurter, now an associate justice on the U.S. Supreme Court, republished his own 1927 book, *The Case of Sacco and Vanzetti: A Critical Analysis for Lawyers and Laymen*. Francis Russell wrote *Tragedy in Dedham* in 1962. He said in the foreword to a 1971 reissue that his belief in Sacco and Vanzetti's innocence began to waver as he completed his earlier manuscript. Russell followed up with *Sacco and Vanzetti: The Case Resolved* in 1986, in which he quotes Moore, Tresca, and Felicani as saying that Sacco was guilty but Vanzetti was not. Other books continue the debate and reflect the passion the issue still evokes, more than seventy-five years later.

BIBLIOGRAPHY

Avrich, Paul. *Sacco and Vanzetti: The Anarchist Background*. Princeton, N.J.: Princeton University Press, 1991.

Ehrmann, Herbert B. *The Case That Will Not Die: Commonwealth vs. Sacco and Vanzetti*. Boston: Little, Brown, 1969.

Feuerlicht, Roberta Strauss. *Justice Crucified: The Story of Sacco and Vanzetti*. New York: McGraw-Hill, 1977.

Fraenkel, Osmond K. *The Sacco-Vanzetti Case*. New York: Russell & Russell, 1931, 1969.

Frankfurter, Felix. *The Case of Sacco and Vanzetti: A Critical Analysis for Lawyers and Laymen*. New York: Universal Library, 1962.

Joughin, Louis, and Edmund M. Morgan. *The Legacy of Sacco and Vanzetti*. Princeton, N.J.: Princeton University Press, 1948, 1978.

Montgomery, Robert H. *Sacco-Vanzetti: The Murder and the Myth*. New York: Devin-Adair Company, 1960.

Porter, Katherine Anne. *The Never-Ending Wrong*. Boston: Little, Brown, 1977.

Russell, Francis. *Sacco & Vanzetti: The Case Resolved*. New York: Harper & Row, 1986.

Russell, Francis. *Tragedy in Dedham: The Story of the Sacco-Vanzetti Case*. New York: McGraw-Hill, 1971.

The Sacco-Vanzetti case; transcript of the record of the trial of Nicola Sacco and Bartholomeo Vanzetti in the courts of Massachusetts and subsequent proceedings, 1920–7. New York, H. Holt & Company, 1928-29.

Sinclair, Upton. *Boston: A Documentary Novel of the Sacco-Vanzetti Case*. Cambridge, Mass.: Robert Bentley, 1978.

Weeks, Robert P. *Commonwealth vs. Sacco and Vanzetti*. Englewood Cliffs, N.J.: Prentice-Hall, 1958.

Young, William, and David E Kaiser. *Postmortem: New Evidence in the Case of Sacco and Vanzetti*. Amherst: University of Massachusetts Press, 1985.

INDEX

Note: Bold numbers indicate pages with photographs or drawings.